D0829566

DISCARDED

I Love You
to God and Back

DISCARDED

DISCARDED

DISCARDED

I LOVE YOU
TO GOD AND BACK

A MOTHER AND CHILD CAN FIND FAITH AND
LOVE THROUGH BEDTIME PRAYERS

AMANDA LAMB

THOMAS NELSON
Since 1798

NASHVILLE   DALLAS   MEXICO CITY   RIO DE JANEIRO

© 2012 by Amanda Lamb

All rights reserved. No portion of this book may be reproduced, stored in a retrieval system, or transmitted in any form or by any means—electronic, mechanical, photocopy, recording, scanning, or other—except for brief quotations in critical reviews or articles, without the prior written permission of the publisher.

Published in Nashville, Tennessee, by Thomas Nelson. Thomas Nelson is a registered trademark of Thomas Nelson, Inc.

Unless otherwise indicated, Scripture quotations are taken from the HOLY BIBLE: NEW INTERNATIONAL VERSION®. © 1973, 1978, 1984 by International Bible Society. Used by permission of Zondervan Publishing House. All rights reserved.

Thomas Nelson, Inc., titles may be purchased in bulk for educational, business, fund-raising, or sales promotional use. For information, please e-mail SpecialMarkets@ ThomasNelson.com.

Library of Congress Cataloging-in-Publication Data

Lamb, Amanda.
  I love you to God and back / Amanda Lamb.
    p. cm.
  ISBN 978-1-4002-0391-8
  1. Christian children—Prayers and devotions. 2. Children—Religious life. 3. Daughters—Religious life. 4. Mother and child—Religious aspects—Christianity. I. Title.
  BV265.L36 2012
  242'.62—dc23   2011042980

Printed in the United States of America

12 13 14 15 16 QG 5 4 3 2 1

DISCARDED

To Chloe, for helping me to become a better person
and for showing me the light one prayer at a time

DISCARDED

CONTENTS

DISCARDED

PROLOGUE

"I love you more than anything else in the whole entire world," I said, leaning in to hug my youngest daughter, Chloe, who was snuggled up in her covers. I could feel a halo of small stuffed animals surrounding her tiny head. Her damp hair smelled fresh, like baby shampoo. I could barely make out her face beneath the glow of her night-light that flashed psychedelic colors across the walls. It wasn't very soothing to me, but she insisted on using it.

"I love you more," she said in her tired, husky voice. Both of my daughters have voices that make them sound like lounge singers who have been singing all evening in a smoky nightclub.

"How much more?" I asked, punctuated by a chuckle, not really expecting her to answer.

"I love you to God and back," she said as a blue light washed across her cherubic face. I could barely see her sleepy eyes and wide grin.

"Wow, that's a lot," I replied, trying to imagine how a five-year-old would come up with such a great way to describe the depth of her love. In her mind, God resides "up there" in the clouds as she has told me on several occasions, pointing to the sky with her head bent forward like Elvis striking his signature pose. To her, the location of God represents the farthest distance she can possibly imagine.

And from that moment on, every night when I left Chloe's room, she would tell me she loved me "to God and back." I couldn't top it, so I didn't even try. I simply told her the truth—that I loved her "to God and back too." As parents, the depth of our love for our children is almost impossible to define or quantify, but Chloe's description was the closest I had ever come to truly being able to express it.

I

ENDLESS SUNSHINE

There shall be eternal summer in the grateful heart.

—CELIA THAXTER

CHLOE: Dear God and Jesus, thank you for getting to have school tomorrow, and getting to have a school year thing that was very fun. Lots of stuff to eat and . . . Help me . . .

MOMMY: What else did we do today? What did we do this morning?

CHLOE: Oh, go out with our friends, get bagels, and eat at their house. Play.

MOMMY: And then what did we do this afternoon?

CHLOE: And they got a new dog. And thank you for letting me go to the pool. Thank you for my family, and one more thing, oh, thank you for Mama!

IN THE BEGINNING

It was Chloe's idea to document her prayers. I had told her that I thought they were so beautiful and that I always seemed to learn something every night when I listened to her pray. I didn't always realize what I had learned right away, but the lesson would come back to me, days later, in small doses when I least expected it. Something simple would happen, such as a stranger holding a door open for me or a redbird pecking at my kitchen window, and I would think, *Chloe would thank God for this.*

Then one night while I was remarking on how special her prayers were Chloe said, "Mommy, why don't you write them down?"

We decided to begin just after her sixth birthday. Documenting the prayers in her Hello Kitty notebook seemed like a good idea at first until we realized that we were sitting in a dark room. That, along with my poor handwriting, convinced me that I needed a more practical option, so I decided to record them. Since I didn't want her to be intimidated or distracted by the voice recorder, I chose a small digital recorder that I could hold at a distance and still get clear sound. I also didn't want her to feel pressure that we would record every single night. We decided our goal within her sixth year was to record one hundred prayers, and then I would transcribe them and make them into a little booklet for her to keep. When she grew up, she would always have this special reminder of her childhood.

"I just talk into it?" Chloe asked me, wide-eyed as I held the tiny handheld recorder near her face. She leaned in thinking she had to have her mouth practically on top of the speaker for it to work.

"You don't have to be that close. Just talk normally. Pretend it's not even there," I said, gently guiding her head back down onto the pillow.

But then something funny happened along the way to reaching our goal. As I listened to Chloe pray every single night, I realized that I was not doing this just for her; I was also doing it for me. I'm a regular mother who wanted to give her daughter a love of God. Yet, with no special skills or theological background, and with as many questions about faith as answers, I felt ill equipped to be her guide. But slowly I started to discover that *she* was *my* guide. Woven in between her simple declarations of thanks and love were trinkets of wisdom about how to approach spirituality, parenting, and life in general. It was only when I stepped back and really started to understand the gift she had given me that I decided I needed to share it with others.

"Is it off now?" she asked that first time we used the recorder.

"It is, sweetie," I replied, tucking it into the pocket of my robe.

"But I've got more to say," she said through a yawn.

"They'll be plenty of time for that, baby. Plenty of time."

CHLOE: Dear God and Jesus, thank you for getting to have a playdate with Julia. Well, Mallory had it today. Thank you for getting to have school today. I'm sad because—well, I'm happy because we're going into first grade, but I'm sad because we're leaving kindergarten. I want to time travel to get all the way to the first grade. My friend Jordan wanted to do that.

MOMMY: So, did you love kindergarten?

CHLOE: Yes!

MOMMY: What are you going to miss about it?

CHLOE: I'm going to miss my teachers, my friends, the whole entire classroom.

MOMMY: Okay, what else do you want to thank God for?

CHLOE: Getting to do swim practice today, and Daddy getting to be home today.

MOMMY: Home early.

CHLOE: Home early. Thank you for my family and one more thing, oh, thank you for Mommy!

SPIRITUAL CORE

Just as some children are born with brown eyes or blond hair, I believe some people are simply born with a deep spiritual core. I might not have recognized it as quickly had Chloe been my firstborn child, but because I already had some experience with raising my older daughter, Mallory, I realized right away that Chloe had an inherent faith that didn't come from Sunday school or her family. It came from somewhere deep within her heart.

"Where did you come from?" I ask Chloe on a regular basis,

meaning it both literally and figuratively, as in, *How did I get so lucky to have such a sweet child?* I am a lot of things, but *sweet* is not a word you would use to describe me—passionate, energetic, intense, but definitely *not* sweet.

"Mommy, God gave me to you. He wanted you to have me, so he brought me down from heaven and put me in your tummy," Chloe always responds.

One day I promised her something—it wasn't a big something, a trip to the park or a movie. I can't recall exactly what it was. But like so many promises busy parents make to their children, she knew there was a chance I wouldn't be able to keep it. She looked me directly in the eyes at five years old and said, "Mommy, you know if you break a promise you will break God's heart."

On this night as we prayed together, her sadness about leaving kindergarten, along with her excitement about starting first grade, was typical Chloe. She has a genuine love for people in her life, like her teachers and friends, and even though she knew there would be new teachers and friends the following year, it was impossible for her to contemplate leaving the old ones behind.

"I wish all of my friends and my teachers could come up to first grade with me," she said.

"I know, baby. They can't, but you will still see them next year," I said, hoping that I was saying the right thing.

"But it won't be the same," she replied, turning away and burying her head in her pillow.

Somehow, though, even in these trying moments, Chloe finds peace in her steadfast faith that allows her to face the challenges in life with God as her copilot. Unlike other children who constantly have to be reassured about God's presence and ask questions to verify his existence, Chloe simply accepted his presence from a very early age. Her strong faith has caused me to question the strength of my own beliefs and tested me in ways that I didn't expect.

"You're right, Mommy," she said after a long silence, lifting her head up from the pillow. "My friends are always in my heart, just like God," she said putting her little hand on her chest in the general vicinity of her heart.

I'd like to take credit for this early spiritual foundation in my daughter, but I'm afraid I can't. Other than having her say a prayer at the dinner table and at bedtime and taking her to church most Sundays, I haven't exactly been a model spiritual leader. I am the kind of mom who occasionally mutters something unsavory under her breath at other drivers or at times pulls out my BlackBerry in church. Yet, somehow, my imperfect soul created this gentle little creature who at the center of her being loves the world and wants what's best for everyone.

"I don't deserve you," I say with a smile when she tells me about God putting her in my belly.

"Yes, you do, Mommy. That's why God gave me to you. He wanted you to have a sweet little girl," she says with absolute sincerity.

She's not perfect by any means; no one is. But she's someone who inspires me every day to be a better person. As parents, we all have moments when the tables are turned and the children become the teachers. When I grow up, I want to be just like her.

CHLOE: Dear God and Jesus, thank you for getting to go to the pool today and getting to go to this party at Cici's house. We got to do five fun things. And Mallory getting to do swim team today. Why are you smiling?

MOMMY: Because you're so adorable, and I can't stand it sometimes.

CHLOE: Help.

MOMMY: What did you guys do on the porch today?

CHLOE: Nothing.

MOMMY: I thought you danced.

CHLOE: No. And thank you for my family and one more thing, oh, thank you for Mommy.

GOD AND JESUS

I've never fully grasped the holy Trinity—the Father, the Son, and the Holy Ghost. Are they one? Are they three? What's the deal? It's a very confusing theological concept. Chloe, however, decided early on that she would not pray to just God, but that she had to pray to Jesus as well. Chloe has actually always had a thing for Jesus—Baby Jesus, that is. From a very early age she started carrying around the plastic Baby Jesus from our nativity scene (which she refers to as "the Jesus house") at Christmastime. It was not unusual to find him in her bed beneath her pillow, in the pocket of her jacket, or even in the bathtub getting a good scrub. At Christmastime, wherever Chloe goes, Baby Jesus goes too.

"Mommy, where's Baby Jesus?" she yelled from her bedroom one day. Immediately, the whole house was on lockdown as we went on a search-and-rescue mission for the tiny Baby Jesus who was inexplicably permanently attached to his manger. I have learned the hard way that when Chloe loses Baby Jesus, we are in crisis mode until he is located.

"Got him," I said as I retrieved Baby Jesus from an empty cardboard paper towel holder that she had hidden behind the giant throw pillows on the couch.

"That's right. I forgot that's where he was. He was napping," she said, snatching the little figure out of my hand and skipping off in the direction of her bedroom.

So when Chloe started saying unscripted prayers, as opposed to "Now I lay me down to sleep," she decided it wouldn't be right just to pray to God. She needed to include Jesus as well. In the beginning of the prayer project, I also said a prayer directly after hers that I did not tape. The idea was that I would also share something special about my day for which I wanted to thank God. Not being a prayer warrior like Chloe, I often found this challenging despite the fact that my only audience was a six-year-old.

"Dear God, thank you for—" I said one night before she cut me off.

"Whoa, whoa, whoa, Mommy. You can't just thank God. How do you think Jesus would feel? It's not right to leave him out," she said, wagging her little finger in my face beneath the glow of the nightlight with its rainbow of groovy colors.

"Okay. Dear God and Jesus, thank you for the sunshine," I said, starting again.

"Sunshine? Mommy. You need something more 'pacific than that. That's not a real prayer," she said, crossing her little arms over her pajamas that were covered in purple monkeys.

"Okay, let's try this again. Can I start from the thank-you part?" I asked nervously.

"Yes," she said impatiently.

"Thank you for getting to go to the pool," I said.

"Done. I used that. You can't use it. You have to use something new," she said incredulously, unfolding her arms and lifting her palms in the air.

"Okay, thanks for the ice cream we had this afternoon," I said.

"Oh, Mommy, I forgot that one. I need to add it in. Can I do mine again?" she pleaded.

That was the last time I said a prayer out loud in front of Chloe. I decided that I was a distraction; plus, I was never very good at unscripted prayers anyway, not even in my head at church. I preferred the ones from the prayer book that I knew by heart. After all, it was Chloe's prayer party, and I was just lucky to be invited. But there was one other guest at the party—it was clear that God was there with both of us.

Chloe on Jesus:

I think he looks like maybe brown hair and I think he has a robe, both of them do. Jesus is the Son of God. He was a teacher, a servant, a healer. He died for us. It shows how much he loves you.

MOMMY: So, it was your last day of kindergarten.

CHLOE: It was more like half a day. We got to give the people who are not coming back next year to first grade a hug and also the teachers. Dear God and Jesus, thank you for letting Mallory have a playdate and I get to go with Clare, and getting to go to a movie and make my own ice cream and getting to make a show with them. Yeah! Thank you for my family, and one more thing, oh, thank you for Mommy!

DAILY BREAD

"Thank you for our daily bread" is a line from a prayer from my childhood. At the time, I had no idea what "daily bread" meant. A literal interpretation would be "food" as the prayer is usually said at mealtimes. But the more I think about it, the more I realize that "daily bread" could stand for all of the little moments in our lives that we take for granted—someone letting you in on a traffic-filled highway, McDonald's bringing back cherry pies, or a found five-dollar bill in the pocket of your just-washed jeans.

Chloe takes very little for granted. She finds moments in every single day to be thankful for—a hug from a friend or a teacher, a playdate, a trip to the movies, homemade ice cream. Somehow, she stores all these little treasures in her brain, and then, in the evening, remembers to thank God for these tiny slivers of joy, no matter how small.

"Can you remind me of the good things from the day, Mommy?" she often asks as she curls up next to me on her bed. Sometimes she needs help remembering, but mainly I think she likes the sound of my voice retelling the highlights of her day.

"You got an extra chicken nugget in your kid's meal at the

restaurant at lunch," I said once, knowing exactly what kinds of things make Chloe smile.

"That *was* a very good thing. You're right, Mommy," she said and rewarded me with a toothy grin.

I wonder if this is a trait unique to children or do we all have this innocent ability to appreciate these seemingly ordinary moments in our lives, but ignore them as we become jaded grown-ups burdened by the pressures that adulthood brings? Are we too caught up in the daily chaos of our lives? Are we so busy answering phone calls, emails, and texts that we aren't capable of noticing the "daily bread"?

I have recently vowed to pay more attention to my "daily bread" with Chloe's help. Today, I thank God for the squiggly pink lines in the sky as the early morning sun peeks over the horizon. I thank God for the way my older daughter, Mallory, doesn't let go of my hand as usual when I reach out for it as we stroll along the sidewalk. I thank God for the crisp apple on the plate in front of me. I thank God for the four rabbits I noticed on my morning walk. But most of all, I thank God for all of the lessons I am learning from Chloe.

—

CHLOE: Dear God, thank you for getting to see Mommy today because she was away. And, Jesus, thank you for having no school and washing my dad's car and our neighbor's car. Going down in our green wagon, and my dad pulling us. And thank you for my family, and one more thing, oh, thank you for Mommy!

MOTHERS, BE GOOD TO YOUR DAUGHTERS

No matter how much time you spend with your children, it is never enough. When my older daughter was a baby, I worked full-time. Eventually, I negotiated a four-day workweek. By the time Chloe came along, I realized that I would need to work less and spend more time at home if I was going to be the kind of parent I hoped to be. This pull, along with my new writing career, prompted me to go to a three-day workweek. But soon, my writing career started to take more of my time at night and on my days off. The cycle of not spending enough time with my girls started all over again. I was right back where I had started.

"Mommy, why are you dressed up?" Chloe asked me one morning.

"Because I have to work today, honey," I responded in a gentle tone.

"But, Mommy, it's *summer.* Why can't you stay home with me?"

I decided I needed to prioritize my family. Work—television reporting and writing—would have to take a backseat. Doing so many things at one time means that I never do anything really well. When I am with my kids, I constantly misplace my BlackBerry that connects me to work. I fight hysteria as I dig through the trash can or a full laundry basket looking furiously for the vibrating albatross that anchors me to the outside world and constantly distracts me from my children. When I am at work, it is not uncommon to get a hysterical call from one of my daughters that she and the babysitter waited for thirty minutes at the piano school only to find out that I had the day wrong. In short, I am far from perfect, but thankfully the screwups are not of the life-and-death variety. I do the best that I can.

Chloe is so thrilled to see me return after a short or long absence that she runs and jumps into my arms with a mile-wide smile. On this particular day, I had returned from an annual overnight trip to a friend's lake house with several women. It was a rare opportunity to connect with friends and recharge the batteries. It was a welcome getaway, but it was still a trip tinged with guilt for a working mother who feels as though she already spends too much time away from her children.

"Mommy!" Chloe yelled, running down the street into the driveway and jumping into my arms before I could even get my bag out of the car.

"I missed you," I said, nuzzling her with my nose in a move she refers to as a "polar bear kiss."

"I missed you too," she said, burying her sweaty red face in between my neck and shoulder.

When I came home, Chloe gave me no guilt trip, just love and sheer joy at my return. She even asked me if I had fun. Her prayer confirmed that she was happy to have me home again. How many of us have envied another person's time away and been unable to be happy at their return because jealousy stood in our way? I know I am guilty of this. Maybe Chloe can give me some pointers. And just maybe her joy at my return will further reinforce my need to be home more than I am in the world. Maybe I need God to pull me along in a little green wagon to remind me that none of us can make the journey alone.

CHLOE: Dear God and Jesus, thank you for getting to go to the pool today and having tryouts tomorrow. You swim, and they see how good you are.

MOMMY: Anything else? Take your time.

CHLOE: Thank you for getting to sleep with Mommy last night, and I hope those people are okay, because that plant exploded and lots of people died. Thank you for my family, and one more thing, thank you for Mommy. The end.

LOVE THY NEIGHBOR

Another one of my childhood prayers ended with thanking God "for everyone in the whole entire world." I think it was a catchall phrase created by my mother to avoid a long list of family and friends I would surely come up with if she had left me to my own creative devices. But Chloe takes this one step further; she gets specific. After Hurricane Katrina, she incorporated praying for the victims into the end of the prayer, a habit that stuck with her for years.

"And, God, please help the hurricane victims," she would say well before she even really knew what the word *victims* meant. She had just heard me say it so many times that it became part of her vernacular at a tender age.

Chloe is big on praying for victims of global natural disasters, but she is also equally focused on praying for people affected by domestic tragedies. Given the fact that I am a local television news reporter, she is privy to more information about these events than most children her age. On this particular day, there was a major explosion at a food processing plant in our area. Several people died, and many others were seriously injured. I had to work late that night, and Chloe wanted to know why. When I told her what had happened, I could tell the little wheels in her head were already turning.

"Mommy, are the people in the hospital going to be okay?" she asked with sadness in her eyes.

"I really don't know, sweetie," I replied wearily after having stood outside in the heat all day long near the explosion site. "We just need to pray for them."

Chloe said a silent prayer for the victims in her head, then made sure to incorporate them into her bedtime prayer. Chloe takes the admonition to "love thy neighbor" seriously.

Every time I say that phrase in church I silently go through a list of people in my head whom I have not loved as myself—the telemarketer I hung up on, the viewer who sent me a critical e-mail, or the salesperson I was short with. I always vow to do better, but each week the list is equally long. This is something I am working on.

As a child, I remember my mother telling me to say a prayer when I saw an ambulance go by because it meant that someone was in pain. To this day, I say a silent prayer in my head when I see one pass with its red lights flashing. I tell my children it is not necessary to always say a prayer out loud; if you are more comfortable saying it in your head, then that's okay.

"Mommy, I just prayed for that person," Chloe will say when the flashing red lights of an ambulance zoom by us on the highway.

"That's good, honey. I did too," I say, thinking how amazing it is that my mother gave me this gift, and now I am giving it to my daughter.

"Do you think God is listening?" she says.

"Absolutely," I reply without hesitation.

People are always talking about the power of prayer and how it really works. I wonder, if we all prayed for victims of natural disasters and tragedies every night like Chloe does, could we help people heal? It would be hard to imagine such a collective force not having an impact. I don't know the answer, but I do know the victims have one powerful little angel on their side. Chloe shows me the heart of God in the way she thinks about others. In these moments it becomes perfectly clear to me why God gives us children—because they are little walking, breathing reminders of his unconditional love.

Chloe on Kindness:

When you're kind to people, they're kind to you back. But God doesn't care if they're kind to you back; he still wants you to be kind to them anyway. You can be kind by very little things like opening a door for someone or giving them a hug. That's kind.

CHLOE: Dear Jesus and God, thank you for letting me do my swim team thing today—tryouts.

MOMMY: What else did you do today? Did you have a playdate?

CHLOE: (*grunts*)

MOMMY: Okay, honey, come on. Do it.

CHLOE: I messed it up.

MOMMY: Well, just think about anything, okay. Are you done? Hurry up. It's ten o'clock. Come on.

(*The struggle continues for another forty seconds. I am tired and impatient because she can't think of anything to say. I am trying to help her, which makes her even more frustrated. Finally, she finishes.*)

CHLOE: Getting to watch *Aladdin*. Getting to read the cool book, *I Think I Love You*. Um, thank you for getting to have a playdate with Taylor.

WHAT I HAVE LEFT UNDONE

This is exactly what I didn't want to happen. I didn't want to coerce my daughter into saying prayers just because I thought it would be a good idea to record them. At the same time, I am by nature a type A person. Once I set my mind to something, I can't let it go. If I ignore it, it weighs me down, creeps into my thoughts in the category of "what I have left undone." I was not about to give up so early in the game on the prayer project despite her newfound resistance, even though it would have been easy to abandon it. After all, this was only the seventh prayer. Ninety-three more sounded so daunting. But the more I thought about it, the more I realized that God was testing me in ways I hadn't been tested before. It wasn't all about

Chloe; it was also about how as a parent I could find the patience to guide her with God's help.

"Mommy, I'm *too* tired," she said before I turned the recorder on. "Can't we just skip it tonight and do it tomorrow?"

"Nope, because then you might forget what you are thankful for today," I replied with my verbal lasso trying to rein her into my way of thinking. "You're on a roll. Let's keep it up!"

I think patience is, and has always been, my biggest challenge in parenting. The methodical, slow pace of a child is so different from the frenetic, blustery pace of my adult life. Yet I know that it is good for her and her sister, and would improve my life, for me to learn how to slow down and enjoy the moment instead of always fixating on what comes next.

With both of my children, I have always been in charge of the bedtime routine primarily because my husband has less patience than I do when it comes to this particular task. But while I am reading the books and listening to the prayers, inevitably my mind begins to wander to what I need to do next—laundry, unload the dishwasher, e-mail, a writing deadline. This prevents me from being in the moment with my children. In addition to being weary after a long day at work, my impatience can turn the nighttime ritual into something tedious that I dread rather than being a peaceful moment of bonding between my daughters and me.

So, after listening back to this "prayer struggle," I decided that I would have to let Chloe go at her own pace as she told her prayers. I would need to allow the pauses and the silences instead of dreading them and trying to fill them. I needed to find a way to appreciate the moment I was sharing with my child, a way to revel in the beauty of something left undone on purpose. I knew it was going to be a journey of ninety-three more steps.

CHLOE: Dear Jesus and God, thank you for getting to play at my aunt Jennifer's, going to their pool, watching Mallory do tennis. And thank you for getting to eat some pizza, and Daddy getting to come.

MOMMY: Is that it, baby? Do you want to say amen?

CHLOE: I'm not saying that word.

MOMMY: Well, you've got to end it somehow.

CHLOE: Thank you for getting to go to the pool, and thank you for my family. And one more thing, oh, thank you for Mommy.

CAN I GET AN "AMEN"?

It occurred to me on this night for the first time that Chloe never said "amen" at the end of her bedtime prayer. She always said it when she prayed at the dinner table or in church, but not at bedtime. For some reason I decided she needed to start saying it—wrapping the prayer up with a neat little bow. Then I began to wonder, why was it so important to me that she say the word, and even more significantly, why was it so important to her that she not say it?

When Chloe was younger she hated saying my version of the traditional bedtime prayer "Now I lay me down to sleep." I had substituted "fly" for "die" in the line "if I should die before I wake," because the thought of a child thinking about dying in her sleep really distressed me. But my editing was the beginning of the end for Chloe on scripted prayers.

"Mommy, I know that's not the right word. I heard you telling Mallory it was really 'die,' but you changed it. I want to say it *my* way," she said.

"What way is that?" I asked a little too defensively.

"The right way." This got me thinking about the tug-of-war between parents and children—between our expectations of them and their need to do things on their own. I always said "amen" at the end of my prayers as a child, so I expected her to do it my way, as if it wasn't really a prayer without that final word. But in her mind it was just one more thing I was telling her to do when what she really wanted to do was create her own version of a prayer ending, which she did. She always thanked God for her family and then squealed "Ohhhhhhhhhh" as if she forgot something. She would put her finger to her forehead like she was trying to remember what she forgot, and then scream, "Thank you for Mommy!"

Early on, I took this as a compliment that I was being singled out in the family for a special mention. But later in the year I realized that if you happened to be in the room when Chloe was saying her prayer, you got a mention. This included her father, Grif, her sister, Mallory, and her grandmother "Maddie."

So I realized that her ending was just as good as the traditional one that accompanied most prayers. Who am I to say how my child should close a conversation with God? I'm sure there will be many things I will weigh in on throughout her life, times when I am sure I know better than she does. But, as parents, we need to start early allowing our kids to make their own decisions. It's not easy, though. I know what you're thinking right now. *Amen, sister. Amen.*

CHLOE: Dear God and Jesus, thank you for getting to have breakfast with my friends and helping us find the new body cream. We've been looking for six years. It was at Whole Foods. And taking a nap with Mommy and getting to go in the sprinkler and getting to go to a birthday party. And thank you for my family, and one more thing, oh, thank you for Mommy!

MIRACLE CREAM

At some point in both of my daughters' lives I started using God to explain all unexplained events. I think this was passed down from my parents.

"Why is it raining?" Mallory asked one day.

"Because God decided the plants and trees needed water," I said confidently.

"Didn't he know I'm in my bathing suit on the way to the pool?" she replied with her little arms crossed and her lips pursed.

It became an easy way to answer the unanswerable questions about the world. I made it clear that God created and managed the universe— the good and the bad. The result: when things didn't go their way, they would blame God, *not* me. But on the flip side, when things went their way, God got the credit, especially in Chloe's world. In her mind there were no miracles too small or too big to put on God's résumé.

On this day we had been to brunch with some friends. I was sharing with my good friend Amy that Chloe's eczema had gotten so bad on her arms that she was scratching all of the time, sometimes to the point of bleeding. Because Mallory had also had eczema, I thought I had tried every remedy under the sun. Amy suggested we try a product at Whole Foods called "California Baby." So we left the restaurant and went right to the grocery store. Amy knelt down in the aisle of the store, gingerly rolled up Chloe's little sleeves, and gently applied the cream to her inflamed skin. Almost immediately, we could see the skin go from red to a lighter pink.

"It's a miracle," I said out loud like someone in an infomercial. Right then and there "California Baby" could have signed me up as their spokesperson. I couldn't help myself; after years of trying dozens of prescription creams and fancy nonprescription creams suggested by doctors, this stuff from the organic grocery store around the corner seemed to be doing the trick. Chloe looked at her arms and glowed.

"It feels better already, Mommy, for real," she said, holding out her arms stiffly as if bending them might halt the healing process.

"I'm so glad, sweetie," I said, hugging her carefully so as not to brush against her rigid arms.

For Chloe, my use of the word *miracle* naturally meant that God was sending the healing. I started to wonder if maybe she was right, if all those things I took for granted, like good health, were really being guided by God on a daily basis. With that in mind, I grabbed four jars of the miracle cream and headed to the register. I decided you can never have too many miracles in the house.

Chloe on Miracles:

A miracle is like when Daddy lost his wedding ring and the big trucks buried it in the sand and made it harder. But he found it after. God is in charge of that.

CHLOE: Dear Jesus and God, thank you for getting to have a swim meet tonight, having my Raleigh School camp, and getting close to Mommy's birthday . . . Help . . .

MOMMY: I think that's good. Why don't you just do your closing part?

CHLOE: What closing?

MOMMY: When you thank God for your family.

CHLOE: How is that a closing? Like closing a gate?

CLOSINGS

Along with a lack of patience, perhaps my next biggest shortcoming as a parent is trying to understand how children think. When I'm tired or in a hurry, I forget that their little brains don't operate the way ours do and sometimes the words we use make no sense to them.

Again, I am a person who likes thing wrapped up in a neat bow at the end of the day. So I always need a beginning, middle, and ending to a project. I'd given up on making Chloe say "amen." Sometimes she would say it and sometimes she wouldn't, but I still needed a clear ending to the prayer. Thinking that Chloe would understand what a "closing" was, was like asking her to talk about the stock market or rebuilding a lawn mower engine.

Children are very literal creatures. We have to teach them about irony, sarcasm, and figures of speech. Chloe, luckily, has always been a quick study at this stuff.

She also has a way of describing something in such a logical way that it makes total sense when I reflect on it. Why not describe the ending of a prayer as "closing the gate"? After all, gates are meant to be closed and then opened again. At night we close the gate to our conscious world. When day breaks, we open it again, letting the world and all of its experiences in. We become weary again at the end of the day, and the cycle repeats itself. The gate opens, the gate closes.

I decided that I would strive to understand Chloe's language better and not always try to make her see things the way I do. Maybe I need to replace my "amen" with a gate.

CHLOE: Dear God and Jesus, thank you for having a good day and having swim team and getting to have no rain and getting to almost be done with our show that we have at the Raleigh School camp, the story camp. And thank you for my family, and one more thing, oh, thank you for Mommy!

THE SUNNY SPOT

How many days in my lifetime have I spent complaining about the rain, the heat, the cold? Too many to count, I'm sure. But it has never occurred to me to thank God for "getting to have no rain." Obviously, when someone gets married and storm clouds loom in the distance, quietly everyone hopes the rain will hold off. But when it does, do we remember to thank God for the perfect harmony of our plans and nature? I don't think so.

For some reason I am so affected by the weather that I spend more time thinking about how it is destroying my good mood than just about any other factor. Gray days equal the permanent blahs for me. Rainy days automatically make me second-guess everything I'm wearing as there are truly no waterproof professional outfits worthy of being worn on the television news. Hot days used to be okay, but as I get older, I find myself ruing them as well as sweat rolls down the backs of my legs into my high heels. But cold days are the worst. I am already perpetually chilly, and in the wintertime I can't wear enough layers.

I spend a lot of time outside in my job as a television reporter, and that probably contributes greatly to my disaffection with extreme weather. While I am quick to complain to God about unpleasant weather, I need to remember to thank him when we have those perfect

North Carolina days—sunny, blue skies, temperate. And we have *a lot* of them.

Chloe recently told me on the beach one day that if there is a ray of sunshine peeking through a cloud, you should smile at it and that will give it the strength to push the clouds away.

"It really works, Mommy. Watch," she said as she stood there in her little green and blue fringed bikini, her tummy bulging and eyes squinting as she looked directly into the sunny spot. The lifeguard overheard her explaining the process to me and stopped to help. He stood next to her at attention like he was in military formation, his hands at his side, and stared at the spot with her.

"Is it working?" he said, talking out of the side of his mouth to Chloe, but keeping his eyes firmly on the spot.

"Yes, yes!" she said as the ray seemed to push a little harder through the clouds and break through with a little more intensity.

I fell in beside them, figuring why not? All my complaining about the weather over the years had gotten me absolutely nowhere. Maybe I was going about it all the wrong way. Maybe God just wanted a little smile and some thanks for the sunshine. As the lifeguard, Chloe, and I continued to stand at rapt attention, I could feel his warmth.

CHLOE: Dear Jesus and God, thank you for getting to go to the pool twice today for swim team and thank you for practicing my play—it's going to be tomorrow. Thank you for letting me read books and getting to go have ice cream, and thank you for my family, and one more thing, thank you for Mommy. Amen. (*In the background I can hear Mallory arguing with her dad.*)

LOVE AND WAR

"You treat her like a little princess," Mallory yelled in the background through the bedroom wall she shares with Chloe's room. "You don't love me the same."

Sibling rivalry has been one of the most baffling aspects of parenting for me. I grew up with an adopted brother five years my junior who spent the majority of his life in boarding school. I also have a stepsister who is twelve years younger than I am with whom I shared a home for exactly one year before going off to college. In many ways I am an only child, so the concept of these two beautiful creatures always egging the other one on is something I sometimes feel completely unequipped to deal with.

Oftentimes, they are the best of friends. Mallory is a good leader, and Chloe is a good follower. You would think this would be a perfect combination, but throw in a little rivalry over my attention and we're talking World War III.

"Mommy, I'm being very good, aren't I?" Chloe asked me with syrupy sweetness dripping from every syllable. Mallory had just stomped off after I failed to address some perceived wrong that was done to her by her little sister. Chloe likes to capitalize on moments when she thinks her self-appointed status as "the sweet one" will get her extra praise or attention.

As soon as I started the prayer project with Chloe, I knew Mallory might get upset that I was concentrating so much on her little sister. However, I had written another parenting book that primarily focused on Mallory several years earlier. Mallory was very proud about being featured in the illustrations I would share from our lives. Since she doesn't like to pray out loud, I assumed she wouldn't care much about my project with Chloe. How wrong I was.

I'm not sure what started the argument that particular night, but my husband, Grif, had clearly sent Mallory to her room for some kind of inappropriate behavior. While Chloe and I were praying, he entered Mallory's room to discuss whatever had transpired. Amazingly, Chloe managed to plow on through the prayer despite her sister's unfiltered rant through the wall. Actually, I think she plowed through it to spite her sister. But I am learning not to fall into this trap when Chloe's looking up at me with her dazzling blue eyes, pouty lips, and seemingly innocent face, trying to win my undivided attention by showing me stellar behavior in the face of her sister's tantrum. I tell her that her sister's meltdown is none of her business, and she needs to stay out of it.

So the prayer on this night left me feeling torn. I needed to finish with Chloe, but my heart was in the other room with Mallory. I could understand what she was feeling. For now, as the younger one, her sister is often going to get more attention by necessity. And while Mallory is turning into a beautiful, talented, bright young woman, Chloe is still a cute, engaging little girl. I found myself silently answering Mallory through the wall. *Chloe is not the only princess in the house. You were my first princess, and will always be my princess. I love you. I love you. I love you. God, please help me figure out how to make her believe me.*

"Mommy, do you want to say a prayer?" Chloe asked when she was done.

"No thanks, sweetie. I already did."

CHLOE: Dear God and Jesus, thank you for getting to roller-skate at my friend's party and having Father's Day today and having a sleepover last night with Cici and her big sister Livi and getting the diving board necklace. I thought I would get a green one. There's green, red, and white, and I got a white one. And thank you for my family, and one more thing, oh, thank you for Mommy!

WITH GOD'S HELP

Things have not always come easily to Chloe. She is a very hard worker. Her teachers have always said that if they tell Chloe to go back and redo something she will put her entire heart into it. When Mallory is successful at something in school or in an extracurricular activity, it is the norm. She is a child whom God blessed with brains, athletic prowess, and creative abilities. Chloe, on the other hand, possesses talent as well—especially artistic talent—she just has to work a little bit harder than her sister to succeed sometimes.

I was not a naturally athletic child, although as an adult I am fiercely into fitness. But when teams were picked in gym class, I was usually chosen last. As I got older and was forced to play team sports at my small religious private school, I spent a lot of time warming the bench and nursing my bruised ego. While Mallory somehow inherited her paternal aunts' athletic DNA, as well as their long legs, Chloe, unfortunately, inherited my DNA, which appears to be hopelessly deficient in the hand-eye coordination department.

"Mommy, I can't run until I get some water," she said defiantly one morning. She was participating in a neighborhood road race for kids. I jogged slowly next to her just outside the course boundaries to give her support. She had not only stopped running, but had slowed to a pace that was almost impossible to match without feeling like you were moving in slow motion.

"You can do it, sweetie," I said as I jogged backward in place so that I could face her as I waited for her to catch up. I was regretting my decision to allow her to participate in the race, but she had begged me to let her do it.

"I need air condition," she said as I heard Grif yelling to her in the distance to run.

Chloe gets hot and overwhelmed easily by too much physical activity. Her little round face turns bright red, and I often turn around on a bike ride to see her off her bike, her tiny arms crossed, and a pout peeking out beneath her pink bike helmet. She knows where all of the benches are on our route and likes to stop frequently for "breaks." So, when she told me she wanted to take the test to be able to use the diving board and slide at the neighborhood pool, I was more than a little skeptical. But she had spent day after day at the pool watching her sister and their friends gleefully jump off the diving board and race down the slide squealing with joy. In order to be allowed to do this, kids had to pass a swimming test. They had to swim two laps without stopping to touch the bottom or hold on to the side. If they passed, they got a waterproof necklace that showed the lifeguard they were permitted to play in the deep end of the pool.

"Mommy, it's not fair. *Everyone* gets to go off the diving board but me," she said to me practically every day we went to the pool.

"Sweetie, you have to be big enough to pass the test. You're just not ready yet," I would say as gently as I possibly could.

Grif was sure Chloe could do it. I was not so positive. This was her first year on swim team, and she was barely able to swim a lap without stopping. I pictured her sinking underwater halfway through the test as we sat on the edge of the pool screaming at her to continue. In seconds I would be in the pool, doing yet another water rescue, something I had already mastered many times in my children's short lives.

But her determination to get the necklace, to swim in the deep end with her sister, proved too strong for my doubts. I agreed to let her try the test. Grif, Mallory, and I watched nervously as she struggled to make it through that first lap. Her blue goggles pinched her face in such a way that her eyes bulged out like an octopus every time she lifted her tiny head out of the water. Kids always look like they're drowning when they are learning to swim, and Chloe was no exception. Her short legs frantically kicked, while she alternately doggie paddled and did a rudimentary version of the breast stroke. For her second lap she chose the backstroke—what she refers to as her "best stroke." Somehow she managed to keep herself for the most part inside the lane, although she zigzagged some, bumping into the rope a couple of times. All I could see were her toes, her round belly, and her tiny arms coming up out of the water. But as she got closer, the grin on her face as her fingers hit the wall was price-less. She whipped off the goggles, which left big red rings around her eyes. Her hair was matted and standing up in clumps around her pale, white face.

"Did I do it?"

"Yes, you did it!" all three of us cried simultaneously.

Grif walked Chloe over to the lifeguard where she was awarded her necklace. Not a green one like her sister's, but a white one. She walked back to the side of the pool where I was sitting and proudly displayed it to me. Quietly, I chastised myself for not believing she could really do it. But, in my heart, I knew that Chloe possessed a determination that would get her very far in life even if she didn't always possess raw natural talent in a given area.

"Mommy, why do you think I got a white one instead of a green one like Mallory?" she asked.

"I don't know, honey, maybe they ran out of the green ones," I replied.

"Nope. I think you get a special one for doing the backstroke," she said proudly. I nodded in agreement, but silently I thought there *was* something symbolic about her getting the pure white necklace. I reminded myself that as parents even when we may momentarily doubt our children, God does not.

CHLOE: Dear God and Jesus, thank you for getting to go to the pool and getting ribbons. I'm the only one who got three ribbons, I think. Going to the house with the horses and getting to see squash, tomatoes, and corn and real stalks, maybe five feet tall. And thank you for my family, and one more thing, thank you for Mommy. Amen!

All God's Creatures

Chloe is an animal lover. I don't mean she simply likes to pet cute puppies that pass by us; I mean she gets down on her knees, strokes them gently, and looks into their eyes. I, on the other hand, am not what you would call an animal lover. Don't get me wrong. I've had pets off and on my entire life. I don't dislike them. I'm just not drawn to cute, fuzzy creatures the way Chloe is. So I am constantly amazed by her absolute joy when she meets a new animal—a dog, a cat, a baby chick, you name it. She loves them all equally.

"Mommy, we played with the chickens at Camryn's house today," she told me one day after a playdate.

"Really, what was that like?" I said, thinking how playing with chickens is about the last thing on earth I would ever want to do.

"Good. I picked them up. They all have names," she said, miming how one picks up a chicken with both arms.

I've gotten to the point now where I constantly point out animals to her everywhere we go, animals that used to be invisible to me.

"Look at that cute dog, Chloe," I'll say. She will immediately run up to the dog and its owner, hoping they will both be friendly. I also hope they will be friendly. Luckily, most of the time they are, but I have taught her to always ask the owner before petting a dog just in case they are not.

"Mommy, can I go pet him? Can I?" she asks as she jumps up and down and pulls my arm in the direction of the dog.

"Girls, look at all the sheep in that field," I say as we whiz past a farm. Chloe excitedly presses her nose to the glass, while Mallory shrugs and keeps on reading her book. Mallory has my animals-are-just-okay gene.

When there's an opportunity for Chloe to see animals, we jump at the chance. Grif has a friend with a small farm and so on this particular day he took the girls to see the animals. Grif has always been allergic to any animal with hair, especially horses. When he was a child he recalled his grandfather's disappointment that he could not ride the ponies on his farm. But Chloe can stroke their soft manes and feed them carrots and apples without sneezing or breaking out in hives like he did. She would stand there for hours if you let her, transfixed by their beauty. Given the fact that a real horse is not in our future (we have plenty of stuffed ones), I am more than happy to let her enjoy other people's horses.

I was not surprised that Chloe thanked God for seeing the horses. I was a little surprised that squash, tomatoes, and corn also made their way into the prayer. But then it hit me: *Chloe has never seen where real food comes from. She thinks it comes from the grocery store, and more often than not, from a can, a bag, or a box.*

As she closed her eyes that night, I rubbed her head, brushing the wisps of blond hair off her forehead. She had a stuffed polar bear in one arm, a stuffed pink poodle in the other arm, and an assortment of small stuffed monkeys held together in a chain with Velcro on the pillow surrounding her head. Above her on the wall next to the bed was a framed print my mother had given me called "Noah's Ark," dimly lit by the night-light. I got the message loud and clear. To be Chloe's mom I was going to have to learn to love all God's creatures.

CHLOE: Dear God and Jesus, thank you for going to Maddie's and Pop Pop's, and thank you for getting to see fireworks, and thank you for getting to see Baby Will, and thank you for getting to have cupcakes and chocolate muffins and one more thing, oh, thank you for Mommy. Amen.

LIGHT OF MY LIFE

I love it when Chloe thanks God for people other than her immediate family. On some nights she thanks God for everyone in her family, "including the people who don't live with me."

This prayer fell in the middle of our annual summer vacation to the Jersey Shore with my parents. Because I grew up in Philadelphia, we spent many summers visiting the shore, and now my children are carrying on this tradition. From walking the nearly two hundred stairs to the top of the Cape May Lighthouse to playing the same miniature golf course with the impassable windmill hole to getting cones piled high with soft ice cream dipped in sprinkles, they love the familiarity of this yearly sojourn north. It's also the only time of year that my parents—my mother, Madeline (Maddie), and my father, Bill (Pop Pop)—along with my stepmother Pat (Nonni), get an opportunity to spend quality time with my children.

Despite the distance, I have vowed to make a valiant effort for my children to know my parents. There is something so divine and pure in the relationships that skip generations. Not only are grandchildren little genetic reminders of their grandparents, possessing undeniable family traits, but there is an undeniable connection between children and grandparents defined by an unconditional love that flows freely in both directions.

"Mommy, can Pop Pop come over tomorrow?" Chloe asked me one night.

"No, sweetie, he lives a long way away," I said to her as her lips formed a pout.

"But, Mommy, he said it only took an hour to get here," she said, palms in the air.

"By plane, honey, by plane," I said, pulling her to my chest for a hug.

"Oh," she said, her voice muffled as she spoke into the lapel of my robe.

On this night of prayer, as Chloe drifted off with a permanent smile on her sleeping face, I asked God to remind me of this joy she got from knowing her grandparents. I was very surprised that on July Fourth Chloe rated seeing her grandparents higher than seeing fireworks. For most six-year-olds fireworks take center stage. But clearly, her *grandparents* light up her life even more.

Chloe on Grandparents:

You feel *so* excited when you see them!

CHLOE: (*Praying with Daddy.*) Dear God and Jesus, thank you for getting to have dinner with my family and getting three library books and I can read all of them. And thank you for getting to go to the pool with my friends Cici and Brooke, and we met a new friend. And we're going to have a yard sale—that's a fun part. And getting Maggie [the dog] to have a haircut. She's so tiny. And getting my room to be cleaner, and thank you for my family, and one more thing, oh, thank you for Daddy. Amen.

DADDY'S GIRL

When I see one of my girls asleep in my husband's arms as he carries them from the car into the house, I am reminded of my own father. I remember being a little girl and thinking that my father was invincible; that as long as I was with him, I was safe. I now see my girls look at Grif with that same unbelievable feeling, that he is their hero. It sometimes moves me to tears. I'm such a softy, honestly, but I can't help myself. There really is nothing like the adoration a little girl has for her father, and to see my daughters so completely convinced that their father is their rock, their protector, their everything, is just about as sweet as it gets.

My generation of women saw our fathers at the dinner table and at the occasional school event, and that was about it. Our mothers did most of the child-rearing and our fathers worked. Even the mothers who worked also did the majority of child-rearing. Today's fathers are so much more involved with their children, and their children are better for it. They say that girls get their sense of confidence and self-esteem from their fathers, and that if their fathers treat them with respect, they will demand respect from the men they meet in their lives. I know my girls get a lot of love from their father, but more importantly, they get that sense that they are the center of his universe. He may not always have the words to express his love the way I do and he may not always understand them the way I do; but, by his actions, they know that Daddy is always there for them and loves them without question.

Traditionally, I had done the prayer with Chloe. But I decided one night that Grif should give it a try. I showed him how to use the digital recorder and sent him armed with it into her room. Of course, Chloe was so excited to have him there that she showed off for him. Her prayer was full of laughter and bravado as if she wanted to prove that praying every night was really fun and that he should come back for more.

Unlike me, the type A mother, he didn't try to keep her on track, so her thoughts jumped from one random place to another. I knew when I listened to it afterward that he was probably getting a bit impatient. But I was proud that he managed to hold it together and let her do her thing without interrupting like I often do. Listening to their prayer together also reminded me how important it was to allow Chloe to follow her own heart instead of my mental outline.

My favorite part was that she thanked God specifically for her dad that night. This was when I realized that Chloe is all about loving her family equally and being fully present with the goodness God puts in front of her.

CHLOE: Dear God and Jesus, thank you for getting to go to the pool today even though it was lightning, and getting to play with my friends, and getting to go to mini-golf, and winning some games, getting a parachute girl and a ring, getting to mow the lawn with Daddy. And thank you for my family, and one more thing, oh, thank you for Mommy. Amen.

Things Great and Small

Chloe has always been attracted to little things—small stuffed animals, small plastic toys, pieces of string, cardboard toilet paper rolls. She carries these small things with her wherever she goes, in her hands or in her pockets. Inevitably, we lose them along the way, which sends her into a frenzy of epic proportions and usually sends me underneath a booth in a restaurant crawling around on a sticky floor in my high heels and suit looking for "Green Man" or "Blue Bear" or a special strand of golden fleece, a.k.a. yellow yarn.

So getting things like "a parachute girl and a ring" means something significant to Chloe. She loves her big toys too, but for some reason the small toys hold a special place in her heart, as if they need protecting more than the giant teddy bear on the rocking chair at the end of her bed. The small items usually congregate on her desk. After several days, the pile gets larger, and I finally have to put some of them in a drawer.

"Where is my parachute girl?" Chloe screamed from her bedroom one day while I was in the kitchen opening mail.

"Not sure, check your desk drawer," I said as I casually flipped through the Pottery Barn catalog, enjoying one moment of respite at the end of my busy day.

"I'm serious. She is special. I neeeeeeeeed to find her," she yelled again.

I ran back to the bedroom and started rummaging through the drawers of her desk. Then it dawned on me: parachute girl had become twisted in her parachute and had to be extricated with scissors. Since she was no longer attached to the plastic chute, I hadn't seen any reason to keep the small character that looked like the dozens of other toys Chloe already had crammed into her drawers.

"You threw it away, didn't you, didn't you?" she said, looking at me with an accusatory glare.

"I'm sure we'll find it," I replied nervously as I continued to rummage through her desk drawers, knowing full well that parachute girl was probably buried several feet down in the local landfill by now.

Chloe knows that I am a first-rate thrower-awayer. I hate stuff, especially small stuff. Every once in a while, I go through her room with a garbage bag and get rid of what I think she won't miss. But I know that I'm always taking a chance when I do this that she might notice *something* is missing. I know I need to take a more hands-off approach to her stuff and allow her to sort through on her own what she really plays with and what she doesn't. But all too often when I give her the task of cleaning out her toys so that we can give whatever she doesn't want to charity, she has trouble parting with anything. After spending literally hours poring over each droopy teddy bear, every cheap stuffed neon animal from the State Fair, and every tiny stuffed animal that she keeps in her pockets until they are threadbare and gray from an unknown source of grime, she usually decides to give away about four out of a hundred.

"I'm sorry, sweetie. I may have accidentally gotten rid of parachute girl. I'll get you another one," I said sheepishly, proud of myself for finally having the guts to own up to my mistake.

"God," she said, looking up. Automatically my eyes went to the same place, maybe hoping to see him hanging out near the ceiling fan. "Please keep parachute girl safe wherever she is. And bring me a new one if you have time."

CHLOE: (*Praying with Daddy.*) Dear God, thank you for getting to go to the pool for a little bit. Thank you for Skye's birthday, my friend. I'm thinking. And getting to get lots of tattoos and make pretend guitars at Skye's birthday, and thank you for my family, and one more thing, oh, thank you for Daddy. Amen.

Rock Star

One of the things I love about Chloe is her ability to suspend disbelief. While her sister is more literal, Chloe has always been into fantasy play. She makes up elaborate stories with her dolls, stuffed animals, and small toys as the main characters. They talk back and forth to one other. She of course makes different voices for each character. Often I think she is talking to me when she is not.

"Mommy, I told you not to go there," I heard her say emphatically one afternoon.

"What? Go where?" I replied.

"I'm not talking to you," she said with an exasperated look on her face. She had about a dozen small toys—dolls and stuffed animals—in a circle around her little wooden castle.

"Oh, sorry, I just heard 'Mommy,'" I said, my words trailing off as I left her to her imaginary play.

On this day she got a chance to go to one of my best friend's daughter's birthday parties. Jodi is one of the most creative people I know. By day, she is an executive at an international technology company. But when Jodi puts on a birthday party, *Martha Stewart move over*. The parties always have a theme that features role-playing and intricate crafts. Jodi honestly has a gift for designing the most engaging birthday parties for children that are unparalleled by any others that I have ever seen. The theme of this particular party was "Rock Star," patterned after Disney Channel characters who miraculously become pop stars as teenagers. The girls dressed up like rock stars, complete with backstage passes and faux guitars that they made. Then they put on a mock show and posed for pictures. It was exactly the kind of birthday party that kids love—especially Chloe, full of make-believe.

Chloe came home from Skye's party that day with glitter on her face, a homemade guitar, and a picture of herself as a rock star hanging around her neck. But it was her smile that told me all I needed to know about the party. I listened from the bedroom doorway in the dim glow of Chloe's night-light as she recited her prayer with Grif. She was so tired from all the excitement of the party that she could barely get the words out. When they were done, I went in to kiss her good night. The glitter from her face had migrated to the pillow in a halo around her little head. She may be a rock star by day, but to me, she looked like an angel.

CHLOE: Dear God and Jesus, thank you for getting to go to the pool and getting to go on a bike ride and thank you for getting to read really, really good books that we haven't read in a long time. And watching the best movie ever called . . . What is it called?

MOMMY: Something about princesses. I don't know. Disney . . .

CHLOE: I need to know.

MOMMY: Go ask your sister. She'll know.

CHLOE: (*She leaves for a moment and then comes back.*) Princess Protection Program. And thank you for my family, and one more thing, oh, thank you for Mommy! Amen.

Sisterly Love

As I said earlier, I didn't grow up with a sister, so I really don't have a handle at all on how siblings connect. But what I do know is that as fiercely as they sometimes seem to dislike each other, Mallory and Chloe love each other just as much. Given that the sibling relationship is likely the longest relationship you will have in your life, I think it is worth protecting. As their mother, my job is to help them work out their differences while somehow maintaining that strong bond of love and shared life experiences.

For all of her toughness, Mallory does have a soft spot for her little sister. They sometimes fight like pro-wrestlers, but at other times, she is very tender and helpful with her little sister. I see the way Chloe looks at her sister, wide-eyed, with excitement and with the hope that she will play with her. When they are engaged in a game together, nothing can tear them apart. When I ask Chloe how she learned something, she inevitably answers, "Mallory taught me."

If I don't know something, Chloe often says, "Let's ask Mallory. She knows everything." So that's why I broke my cardinal rule of a quiet prayer between mother and child and let Chloe get up this night and go ask her sister the name of the movie.

I believe in my heart that God put these two very different girls together for a reason. I believe that Mallory will lead and teach Chloe and give her the courage to do many things she might not otherwise try. Recently, she taught her to knee-board. I thought Mallory was crazy when she suggested my tiny girl who immediately acts exhausted at the mere mention of physical activity would dare allow herself to be pulled behind a boat at thirty miles an hour while kneeling on a board that she is strapped to. But Mallory got in the water with her and patiently showed Chloe how to hold on to the board and pull herself up.

When Chloe finally got up, the proud smile on her face was unbelievable. I looked back at Mallory, who was floating in her life jacket nearby in case Chloe fell. She had the same smile watching her little sister master something we thought she would never be able to do.

"Way to go," I yelled from the back of the boat as I tried to keep the video camera steady to capture the unbelievable moment. Mallory had her hands over her head in the water punching the air with victorious fists.

Chloe, on the other hand, will help soften Mallory's edges. She has a great deal of empathy and understands social nuances in a way that Mallory's literal brain cannot always grasp in the moment. Together, they will be unbeatable. There's no doubt about it. It's God's princess protection program.

Chloe on Sisters:

My sister makes me laugh, she does make me laugh. She would help me if we were in danger. She helps me when I need her. She shares with me. I want to be strong like her.

CHLOE: (*Praying with Mommy and Daddy.*) Dear God and Jesus, thank you for getting to play with my friends Skye and Ayden. And thank you for Mommy making brownies so I can eat them. Are there any leftovers? And thank you for going to see Mallory race. She was the best one. She was the star. That big star right there, she's that. She looked like that big star right there at the race. And I said, "Go, Mallory. Go, Mallory." And I was right there, and Mommy and Daddy were there too. And thank you for my family. And one more thing, thank you for Mommy, Daddy, and Sissy. Amen.

A STAR IS BORN

There are times as a parent when my heart simply bursts. Usually it's when my children have worked hard and overcome obstacles in order to be able to accomplish something. The outcome is really not that important to me. My parents told me this when I was a child, and I didn't believe them. But now I do. I don't care if my children come in first; I just want them to finish what they start and feel a sense of pride at the end for doing their best.

Mallory wanted to participate in the neighborhood triathlon. It involved a four-lap swim, a three-mile bike ride, and a run that amounted to a little more than a mile. Since she had never done anything like this before, and was a child who liked to be good at everything, I was a little worried about her. But she convinced me she wanted to do it and would not get hyper-focused on her results.

On the day of the race, Grif, Chloe, and I waited anxiously on the sidelines as Mallory went through her transitions. We were only able to see her when she ran from the pool and jumped onto her bike and when she parked her bike and headed out to the running course. Chloe stood next to me in the sweltering North Carolina heat holding my hand. She would squeeze it hard when she caught a glimpse of Mallory dashing by.

"There she is, Mommy," Chloe said, jumping up and down. "She's so strong. Could I ever do a race like this?"

"Of course you could, sweetie. Someday," I said, turning my attention to Mallory in her tie-dye shirt rounding the corner on her bike. I was so proud of her for doing something that challenging; I would never have dared to do that at her age.

I knew as I stood there holding Chloe's hand tightly that she, too, would dare to do the same race someday because her sister had gone before her. It made me realize how powerful of a role model Mallory was, and would continue to be, for her little sister.

"Mommy, she's so brave," Chloe said to me, looking up not with envy but with the knowledge that her sister was teaching her to be brave too.

Don't we all need someone to think of us as a star? Chloe is that person for Mallory, and Mallory will also be that person for her. God's love allows us to give this gift to one another, to be shining examples that light is truly in the eyes of the beholder.

CHLOE: I want to sleep with you. No, I want to sleep with you.

MOMMY: Honey, I have to take care of Daddy.

CHLOE: Why can't I help too?

MOMMY: Because Daddy needs Mommy. Say the prayer.

CHLOE: I want to help Daddy too.

In Sickness and in Health

My husband has had two back surgeries. Both times he was down for the count for two weeks. He's not used to being dependent on anyone, and I'm not used to having a third child, so the tension was palpable. The first time we planned it around our Christmas vacation so that he would not be missing anything at work. This was a good and bad plan as it meant that not only did I have to take care of him, but I had to handle all of the Christmas festivities by myself. He was so bored and full of cabin fever that he spent a lot of time on painkillers surfing the Internet with a credit card. I finally had to cut him off after the pool table and the surround sound system arrived at our door.

The second surgery was in the summer of 2009. We planned it for after our annual family vacation with my parents in New Jersey. But in all honesty, there's no good time to take two weeks out of your life. For the most part, Grif is a pretty good patient. He simply asked that I leave him alone and take care of the kids. I also doled out his medicine because I didn't want a repeat of the prior painkiller-induced online shopping spree. Although I will admit that the snooker table makes an excellent surface for wrapping Christmas gifts and folding laundry.

Chloe had so much trouble focusing on her prayer that night because all she wanted to do was be part of helping her daddy heal. In her mind, the best thing she could imagine doing for him was snuggling up next to him in the bed. She is the first person in the family to pat your back when you are coughing or hug you when you stub your toe. She has a great deal of empathy that comes naturally to her. I can only imagine that it comes from God, because it didn't come from me. I have struggled in my life to learn how to show affection with more ease, yet Chloe has opened me up to the possibility of living in a world where kindness is the norm, not the exception. I try to live it, I really do. But I fail more days than I succeed. For example, I have begun letting people merge in front of me on a crowded highway when an accident or construction narrows three lanes into one. After I let the first person in I feel like a saint, but about the time I let the fourth person in (because frankly I'm not sure where to cut it off), I start to get mad at myself for being weak and getting walked all over by aggressive drivers.

Still, observing Chloe's journey gives me hope that there is a God guiding our hearts to do the right thing even when our heads are telling us to do something else. So that night I allowed her to lie in between us and gingerly rub her father's arm while he dozed. I learned in that peaceful moment as I watched Chloe watch her father in the stillness of the night that the desire to help others has a divine healing power that is unbeatable.

2

CHLOE AND GOD
GO TO FIRST GRADE

People see God every day, they just don't recognize him.

—PEARL BAILEY

CHLOE: Dear God and Jesus, thank you for getting to go to Brooke's party tomorrow. Her birthday was not yesterday, but the other day. Getting to go to first grade, not tomorrow, but the next day. And thank you for going on vacation and seeing my grandmother, one of my grandmothers. I have four of them because my mother has a stepmother and my dad has a stepmother. Vi and Grammy, and Nonni and Maddie! She gives me cupcakes all the time, and she will buy me any toy I want. Except for when they are as big as my room. Now, my room is really big. And thank you for my family, and one more thing, oh, thank you for my mommy. Amen!

ALL IN THE FAMILY

Okay, so out of the mouths of babes the truth is revealed. We are a family of four grandmothers. This includes my mother, my stepmother, my husband's mother, and his stepmother. Because all of these women are involved in our lives, they are also involved in the girls' lives. Our first big challenge was doling out names to everyone to avoid confusion for the girls. Having all these grandparents does make for some interesting moments on holidays when we try to include everyone. It makes me feel like a teenage girl again beholden to my parents' custody agreement. But the girls seem to have no issue with having so many grandmothers. It simply means more love and, of course, more treats and presents.

The girls have different and special relationships with all four of their grandmothers, but they probably spend the most time with my mother, who ironically lives four hundred–plus miles away. Maddie spends a great deal of time throughout the year visiting us because she wants to really *know* the girls. I actually think in some ways she is a better grandmother than a mother because she is much more relaxed than she was when I was growing up. Chloe especially has developed a tight bond with my mother. She runs and jumps into her arms whenever she comes for a visit. My mother does spoil my kids rotten, buying them sweet treats that I refuse to have in the house, clothes that I deem inappropriate, and toys they don't need. But Chloe honestly just loves being with my mother.

"Why do you really love Maddie so much?" I asked her when we finished the prayer that night. I thought she might refer back to the tiny chocolate cupcakes my mother plies her with during her visits.

"Because she listens to me," Chloe said without missing a beat. I turned off the light next to her bed as she rolled onto her side and appeared to drift off to sleep almost immediately. I sat there for a moment watching her little chest rise and fall, listening to her soft breathing. I thought about how we all really just want someone to listen to us, and that's why we pray.

CHLOE: Dear God and Jesus, thank you for getting to go to school tomorrow and getting to play with my friends today, and thank you for getting to go to our friend's Brooke's party. It was awesome, and thank you for getting to finally to see Allison again. And thank you for my family, and one more thing, what is that? Oh, thank you for Mommy. Amen. Good night.

MOMMY: Should we do the song one time?

TOGETHER: She loves me, she loves me, she gets down on her knees and hugs me. She loves me like a rock, oh baby. She loves me like a rock, oh baby, she loves me. My mama loves me.

LOVES ME LIKE A ROCK

Okay, so the song is about a boy. I get that, but for some reason it has always reminded me of the way I love my children—with wholehearted devotion. The lyrics of the 1973 pop song by folk music legend Paul Simon are about a boy who says "the devil would call my name," but yet his mother still loves him no matter what. I think this is the way most mothers feel about their children. Unconditional love is the only thing that sustains us through those moments with our kids when we just want to pull our hair out. I believe it is a gift that God gives us the minute we become mothers—a miraculous state of loving someone so completely that the person can fail and still be loved by us. In essence, it is a mirror image of the way God loves us with all our frailties and imperfections. Loving a child helps us understand this concept.

"Mommy, I love you even when you're *mean*," Chloe said to me one night as we snuggled on the couch. At first, I have to admit I was a bit taken aback by her bold statement. But then, as I thought about it, I realized that it was the single most beautiful thing she had ever said to me. She wanted me to know that she loved me even at my worst.

I can't remember the first time Chloe heard it, but when the line "she gets down on her knees and hugs me" emanated from the CD player, I instinctively dropped to my knees and gave her a bear hug around the waist. This was met with squeals of delight from her, and she became obsessed with not only singing the song but our pantomime to the words. So now, it has become "our thing."

"Mommy, you look so funny when you do that," Chloe says, looking at me down on my knees hugging her fiercely around her waist as I sway back and forth to the music.

"I know. It's okay as long as it makes you smile. Do you want me to stop doing it?" I say, looking up with a fake pout.

"No, Mommy," she replies, laughing and tousling my hair with her little hand like I always do to her.

Usually, it ends with us both falling down on the ground and dissolving into giggles. But the truth is that I do love my children that intensely. It's not because I'm a good person; it's because God gives us the grace we need when we become parents to love with a depth greater than we ever imagined. There's no other logical explanation for this phenomenon.

Loving children this way also gives us insight into the way our parents must love us. Until we become parents, it's hard to imagine the depth of our own parents' love for us. It is truly mind-blowing when this realization hits. You think back on what little appreciation you showed for your parents' love while growing up. I remember sitting with Mallory in the nursery in the middle of the night, feeling overcome with love as I looked at her perfect little face bathed in the moonlight coming in through the narrow slits in the venetian blinds. At that moment I was profoundly sad because I realized that *my parents were telling the truth; they did love me as much as they said they did.* Like God's love for us, parents give love wholly without expectations of getting anything in return—no thanks, no accolades, just giving as much as you can and then more because God's love is the template and the source.

Chloe on Mommy:

I love Mommy because she cuddles with me and she protects me. She cooks me meals that aren't the best, but I like them. She's always there when I need her.

CHLOE: Dear God and Jesus, thank you for the first day of first grade, and I'm in ballet I. I think I'm going to Ballet 12, because I think that's as big as you can go because I saw much older people doing it. I got a long way to go, eleven more years I bet until I finish. Once, when I was in kindergarten when I did my recital in ballet when I was wearing the white costume, I saw some kids. They were so fast.

MOMMY: Is this a prayer?

CHLOE: And thank you for getting to have a playdate with Jordan tomorrow after school. Miss Diane, my best friend's mom, she's going to carpool, and we're going to have a playdate and go to the pool. Oh my gosh, it's so awesome. And thank you for my family, and one more thing, oh, thank you for Mommy. Amen!

GIFTS FROM GOD

Chloe is a dancer. I don't mean that she follows steps properly in her ballet class; I mean the kid can dance. It's obvious when you watch her that she feels the music from somewhere deep down in her soul, and then the moves just well up within her like a geyser releasing pressure. She doesn't plan them; she *feels* them. Frankly, ballet is a little boring for her, so I'm working on getting her into other forms of dance where she can really move. Since she was able to walk, we have turned on music in our house and had "dance parties." She went from dancing to seventies funk in diapers to dancing to her sister's iPod in a leotard and a feather boa.

Sometimes she can get a little saucy, but since it's coming from a place of pure joy and creativity, I usually don't rein her in too much when we are in the privacy of our home among family. Watching Chloe dance makes me think about the fact that in life we all truly have passions—things that we are drawn to, things that keep pulling us in a certain direction. If we ignore those talents, those gifts, and the joy and energy we get from pursuing something we love passionately, we will never really be happy. For me it is writing, for Mallory and Grif it is music, and for Chloe it is dancing. We didn't earn these gifts—they are gifts from God. But like a shiny new bike found under the Christmas tree, you can either take care of it, ride it, and enjoy it, or forget about it and leave it out in the rain to rust.

"It's getting *big*, Mommy. You better get in here *fast*," Chloe yelled at me from the other room over the music. "Big" means the chorus is coming and she is ready to show me her serious moves. I sat down on her bed and watched her bounce from one side of the room to the other with a look of serious concentration on her face.

"Wow, great moves," I said, clapping as she whirled like a dervish around the room.

I don't know if Chloe will be a dancer as she gets older, but I know she will always get joy from dancing the same way I get joy from writing, and her father and sister get joy from making music. As a parent, it is my job to make sure she doesn't leave her gift outside in the rain where it will rust and to help her cultivate gratitude for the gift she has received.

Chloe on Gifts from God:

He made me. He gave me the gift of dancing, of music, of art. He gave me a family I love, and they love me.

CHLOE: God, thank you for getting to have another day of first grade, and tomorrow I have a whole day. The first two days we got half. But the fourth graders, which Mallory is in, they have to do a whole day on the first day. And thank you for getting to go to the pool with Jordan after school. She picked me up. Thank you for playing with Brooke and Luke today, and thank you for my family, and one more thing. What is it? Oh, thank you for Mommy. Amen.

Bring It On

The beginning of the school year inspired a silliness in Chloe. At this time of night when she should have been so tired from her long day, she instead got a second wind. This led her to deliver her prayer in a high-pitched singsong voice that practically punctured my eardrums. What amazes me is the sheer *energy* kids have. Not just the physical energy, but the emotional energy. At Chloe's school first graders attend for a half day in the beginning of the first week to get them acclimated to the classroom before they begin full days. Yet she was clearly ready to go full days immediately. Bring it on, she was saying in her prayer. Her enthusiasm for school is something that translates into every aspect of her young life. Can you imagine adults who work part-time saying, "What I really want is a full day. Give me at least eight hours"? Yet this is exactly what Chloe was asking for—*more school*.

"I can't *wait* to go back to school," Chloe says at the end of every summer break. "I'm bored. I want to see my friends."

"So I'm boring you?" I say with a laugh.

"No, Mommy. I'm just *ready*," she replies with a grin.

It made me feel ashamed when I thought about how I dreaded the sound of the alarm clock in the morning—how I just wanted to hit the snooze button and pull the covers back over my head, how I wanted to erase my mind of the constant to-do list that suddenly invaded my brain at the very first sign of wakefulness. Why do we as adults rue the beginning of the workday so much? Why do we say things like, "Just another day in paradise," or "It's going," when people ask us how our day is going?

It makes me think about how the way our day unfolds has a whole lot to do with how we approach it. My grandfather always used to quote the Bible verse, "This is the day the LORD has made; let us rejoice and be glad in it" (Psalm 118:24). As a child, I never truly understood this verse, but now I do. Approach each day with the enthusiasm and excitement of a child, and the joy will come. That's God's promise to us.

CHLOE: Dear God, today was the third day of school. If I were in kindergarten, and she [Mallory] were in third grade again, she would be my buddy.

MOMMY: You love your sister?

CHLOE: I love Sissy.

MOMMY: Why do you love your sister? What's special about her?

CHLOE: Because she's my sister. Just . . . I love her.

MOMMY: What do you like about her?

CHLOE: Because she's my sister. I like her.

MOMMY: Is she fun?

CHLOE: Sometimes.

MOMMY: Is she smart?

CHLOE: Sometimes.

MOMMY: Is she funny?

CHLOE: Sometimes.

MOMMY: Do you like playing with her?

CHLOE: Sometimes. Thank you for my family, and one more thing, oh, thank you for Mommy!

REALITY LOVE

One thing about children that is almost universal is their inability to lie. When asked direct questions, they are usually honest about their answers. Chloe is a very honest child, but she is also clued in to social nuances about how what she says might be perceived.

On this particular night I was leading her down the path to say nice things about her sister. I figured that Mallory, who is usually within earshot, would hear her, and maybe, just maybe, develop a greater understanding for how much her little sister looks up to her and loves her.

But on this night, Chloe wasn't biting. She wasn't about to give me the pat answers I was looking for. She told the truth. Her sister is fun, smart, and humorous "sometimes." This is the truth. When Mallory wants to be, she can be the most engaging child in the room. I've witnessed moments when I walk by her room and catch her speaking tenderly to Chloe, helping her do something she finds difficult, or teaching her how to do something for the first time. But there are also those moments where they are swatting at each other with hands and negative words.

"I know she loves me, even though she isn't always nice to me. Mallory loves me, oh yeah," Chloe sang in her little husky voice at the top of her lungs one night from her bedroom. I walked by to see her on the floor with a bunch of stuffed animals in a circle. She was making outfits for them out of tissue paper and tape.

"Sweetie, why are you singing that?" I said, trying to contain myself from breaking down into a full-throttle hyperventilating fit of laughter.

"Because it's the truth, Mommy," she said, looking up at me wide-eyed and sincere.

I do worry about Mallory's dominance over Chloe sometimes—a function of both Mallory's age and her personality type. As a mother, my natural instinct is to protect Chloe in these negative moments from her sister because she is younger. But as Chloe gets older and more confident, she is better able to stand up to her sister and find more common ground. I am also slowly coming to realize, with Mallory's help, that Chloe is not always the angel, and Mallory is not always the devil. Little sisters can push their big sisters' buttons as well, and it's usually when Mom is not looking. I am learning to try and stay out of their altercations unless it sounds like blood is being shed. Holding back has never been one of my strong points, so truly extricating myself from my girls' disputes is a process I am working on, but have yet to master.

Once again Chloe shows me how God's love shines through her and allows her to love her sister unconditionally in the same way he loves us. But it's not enough to just witness God's grace working through us to wholly love others; we have to believe in it.

CHLOE: Dear God and Jesus, thank you for almost getting to do a play with my friends. And guess what, me and Mallory wrote a song. Hold this. (*She hands her dad the recorder and picks up her mini-guitar and strums a little.*)

DADDY: Get on with it.

CHLOE: Thank you for my family and one more thing, oh, thank you for Daddy, Mallory, and Mommy. Amen.

The Virtue of Patience

One of the most godly things children teach us is the virtue of patience. Whether you are rocking a newborn baby to sleep, rubbing the back of a sick child, or teaching a child to read or tie a shoe, there is nothing fast about it. As adults, we are used to going nonstop until we fall into bed at night exhausted. There is always one more e-mail to send, one more call to return, one more dish to wash or bed to make. But kids don't operate on this same frenetic system. They do things at their own pace.

This lesson has probably been the hardest for me to learn because I thrive on being a doer. I actually feel guilty when I am not doing something productive at work or at home. Downtime is not something I build into my life. But early on, I realized that Chloe is a child who needs downtime in her life, and in many ways her need for this is forcing me to slow down.

"Mommy, I don't like the way you're always rushing me," Chloe says to me almost every morning as we try to get out the door to school and work.

"I'm sorry, baby, we just have to go soon, that's all," I say as I put her lunch box and water bottle in her book bag and try to remember where my car keys are.

"There you go again," she says, hands in the air, as she stumbles half-dressed away from the breakfast table.

On this particular night the recording started out with Grif, Mallory, and Chloe joking around. They each introduced themselves, and then Chloe stopped and started the prayer several times. It was clear that Grif was becoming increasingly annoyed with her lack of concentration, and I don't blame him. He kept telling her to "get on with it." But she refused to get down to business. He later told me how he couldn't imagine how I was able to "make her pray" every night because with him she seemed so disengaged in the process. I told him that I have no problem getting her to pray, which is the truth, but that it didn't happen overnight. Chloe and I had chosen to take a journey together, and we were both committed to seeing it through. It wasn't that he was doing something wrong; it was just that I had learned from doing it for several months consistently that Chloe needed to be the prayer guide, with me as her affable assistant to gently redirect her when we got off course.

I will probably never truly be a patient person, but I do think that Chloe is teaching me how to develop a small modicum of patience one baby step at a time. It is yet another one of God's virtues for us that comes not on demand, but with a steadfast belief that in him all things are possible.

CHLOE: Dear God and Jesus, thank you for getting to go to Red Robin and buy this new toy frog. Say hi! "Hi, I'm learning how to do a summersault." (*She says this in a mock frog voice.*) He doesn't have a name. And thank you for getting to go to Michael's party. He had it at his house. He had a sports party. This boy has this thing that can fly made out of really fragile board, cardboard, and Michael got that for his birthday. He got a red one, and Michael got a blue one. The other boy got a red one. And thank you for eating dinner with them, and Mallory getting a squirrel [a stuffed squirrel from the game machine at the restaurant]. And thank you for my family, and one more thing, oh, thank you for Mommy.

LIFE IS IN THE DETAILS

Most of us are rushing through life at such a breakneck speed that even important details escape us. Where did we leave our phone? What did we have for breakfast? What time is our child's dentist appointment? That's why most parents, like me, have huge wall calendars or dry-erase boards to keep our hectic schedules straight. These, in addition to our electronic calendars that conveniently remind us with a series of beeps of our schedule in case we forget to look at the wall calendar, are designed to create order out of chaos—controlled chaos being the end result.

Children have no such clutter in their lives that prevents them from retaining details. Thus, they are not only available to observe the most minute details, but they store them in their little brains like precious gems in a jewelry box that they can take out again and again and wonder at their magnificence.

For Chloe, what fascinated her the most about her friend's birthday party were the little cardboard airplanes that had mesmerized the boys. Being in a mostly girl house, Chloe rarely plays with, or even sees, traditional "boy toys." Early on in my daughters' lives I bought a few boy toys thinking that it was important for me not to assume they only wanted girl toys. For many years now, the train set, the blocks, and the Legos have all gathered dust in my playroom. Instead, my girls play dress up and put on shows on our ministage. They play with Barbies and the art supplies. They don't play with the boy toys, which I have been begging them to let me give away.

"Nope, Mommy, I might want to build something with those blocks someday," Chloe says as she preens in front of me in a purple sequined belly dancer costume that is inexplicably paired with a bright red clown nose and a magician's top hat.

At the party, Chloe observed with the curious concentration of Jane Goodall observing apes as the boys threw their planes into the air and watched them soar and eventually crash into a wall, a piece of furniture, or the ground. I actually felt a slight sense of guilt that I hadn't allowed her to explore an interest in boy toys. I also realized that I generally don't allow toys I think are cheap and might fall apart—like toy airplanes—but that maybe it's okay to occasionally indulge my children in such pleasures.

Chloe reminds me that if I don't pay attention to the details, I might miss something important, something God wants me to see. I don't mean missing something like a meeting or a doctor's appointment, but missing something like a guy walking down the street wearing a banana suit for no reason, or a cloud that looks like Elvis, or the return of the pumpkin spice latte to the local coffee shop.

"I am in a comfortable moment, Mommy," Chloe said to me one afternoon when I asked her to do something. She was lying on the floor wrapped in a blanket with her dolls around her. "I love these moments. I don't want to miss them."

I was flabbergasted by her wisdom. Thanks in part to Chloe's keen sense of observation, I am now trying to gather these details every single day and file them in my brain for future reference like the gems they are. And I'm also realizing that it's okay to occasionally hold on to things a little bit longer even when they seem to have outgrown their usefulness. *Even boy toys.*

CHLOE: Dear God and Jesus, thank you for playing with my friends, Mallory being weird. Everyone clap for Mallory (*clapping*). And thank you for Pet Shop Kitty, a weekend, and getting to play on the Wii and getting my nails painted with a butterfly and a flower. And thank you for my family, and one more thing, oh, thank you for Mommy and Sissy.

MALLORY: (*Through the wall from her bedroom.*) Aw shucks, Chloe, I'm flattered.

CHLOE: Amen.

CLOWNING AROUND

No one makes Chloe laugh as hard as her big sister does. No matter what I do or say, I can't make Chloe guffaw the way she does when Mallory is around. Mallory knows exactly what silly things to do and say to send Chloe into fits of uncontrollable, guttural laughter. It is as if they share a special language that only the two of them understand. On one hand, it drives me crazy because it makes it harder for me to get things done when they are acting wild together; on the other hand, I love to see the mutual joy they share when they are laughing together. It is much better than the mutual disdain that swirls like a black cloud around their little heads when they are fighting.

On this night, Chloe could barely breathe because Mallory was making little side comments in the background that were cracking her up. Chloe was beside herself, trying to stay on track with me as I prodded her along, while Mallory tried her best to derail the whole thing, albeit with good humor. I think my ability to keep from interrupting these silly moments is an important part of my journey toward allowing them to develop a relationship without my constant intervention. I am not quite there yet, but I am learning that, with God's help, I can help them create a bond separate and apart from their bond with me.

Chloe calling Mallory "weird" is actually the epitome of a compliment because they both learned in school that "weird" is good because it means "different," and being different is good because it means you think for yourself and don't follow the crowd. They learned this from some very wise teachers.

"Mommy, it's good to be weird," Chloe told me after school one day. "For real, my teacher told me so."

On this night I could tell that beneath the humor, there was a growing admiration between my daughters—that divine inspiration that comes from people who share the same blood was at work. They made each other feel special, just the way God had intended it.

CHLOE: Dear God, God and Jesus, thank you for getting to have homework today. We have to have it once a week, so that's not much homework, that can get really boring. In kindergarten we used to have a lot of really fun work.

MOMMY: You'll get more work. Anything else?

CHLOE: And thank you for having really, really, really, really, really, really good books.

MOMMY: You have to get up on the bed. Keep moving over until you are all the way in the bed. You're going to fall out in the middle of the night. This is bad. You've got to move all the way over.

CHLOE: Mommy, I can't sleep with this big stuffed animal in my face.

MOMMY: Let's move him. Let's finish the prayer.

CHLOE: And thank you for getting to play the Wii today. It's been fixed for a long time. And thank you for my family, and one more thing, oh, thank you for Mommy.

DRIVEN TO DISTRACTION

My tone on this night was annoyed. I was so hyper-focused on Chloe lying in the bed properly that I wasn't really listening to what she was saying. This is not an uncommon trait of busy, tired parents, but in that distraction it's easy to miss the precious moments that feed our souls.

I think about how she wanted more homework. It was early in the school year, and her first-grade teacher was trying to ease her students into a routine, instead of overwhelming them in the first few weeks of school. But Chloe was raring to go. She looks at homework like a badge of honor that she is really becoming a big girl like her sister. Can you imagine thanking God for allowing you to do more work?

"Thank you, God, for allowing my boss to pile on more projects today so that I am even more buried and behind in my work. Please let him give me even more to do," the prayer might go. "And, God, if you get a chance, really throw a wrench into everything, like the flu, a flat tire, or a lost wallet, something to really make me have to work harder than normal to get through my day. Amen."

Just the fact that she was thanking God for work and wanted more makes me realize that maybe we do need to be thankful, not necessarily for the work itself, but for our continued ability to do it and to do it well. I know that I am the happiest when I am the busiest. The more I have on my plate, the more I accomplish. And there is an inherent satisfaction at the end of the day in getting it all done. Like climbing a mountain, sometimes at the beginning of the day my schedule looms large in the distance. I can't imagine how I'm going to fit everything in, but somehow I do it. I end up coming down the other side of the mountain exhausted, but satisfied. Sometimes, when I stand at the top of the mountain and look back at what I've accomplished, I can't believe I've packed so much in and overcome so many obstacles to get to that point.

So thank you, God, for allowing me with your support to do what I do every day. And one more thing: Can you please tell Chloe's teacher that she's ready for more homework?

CHLOE: Dear God, thank you for getting to read good books again. And thank you for Connor and Brooke going to school, so we all go to school now. And guess what, Matthew goes to kindergarten now, and he has a real backpack. (*She says this last part with envy in her voice.*)

MOMMY: You go to different schools. They have different rules. You're not allowed to carry one in first grade.

CHLOE: Yeah, but other kids have rolling backpacks.

MOMMY: Do you want to finish the prayer? Or do you want me to turn this off?

CHLOE: I want to finish the prayer. Thank you for my toy motorcycle being charged so I can ride it. It goes so fast. And thank you for having a good day of school. And thank you for my family, and one more thing. What is it? Oh, thank you for Mommy. Amen, yeah.

A CAMEL THROUGH THE EYE OF A NEEDLE

One of the hardest life lessons to teach children is accepting why some people have certain things that they do not have. Taking this concept one step further, children also have to reconcile why some kids get to do certain things that they don't get to do. When they were very little, my answer was always, "That's the way our family does it. Don't worry about what other people do." But that doesn't seem to fly quite as well anymore now that they are older.

The longer I live, the more I realize that not having everything you want builds character. My daughters share a tiny bathroom in a narrow hallway that connects their small bedrooms. As they become teenagers, I know this space will feel infinitely smaller with the addition of endless primping that young girls do in a bathroom. But I truly believe it will be a good experience for them to have to navigate through and coexist in a small space together.

Their school does not allow backpacks until second grade because totes are easier for the teachers to put papers in and check for items being brought back to school. Totes also take up less room than backpacks do in the small hallways that connect the classrooms. By second grade, the hallways are wider and the students are in charge of their own paperwork and, thus, are allowed to have backpacks. So being that her mother is a rule follower, Chloe must use a tote until second grade.

Ironically, even though they have no textbooks in elementary school, somehow the children load their backpacks down with so many notebooks and library books that they eventually need to graduate to rolling backpacks.

Chloe really isn't a child who wants for much, and most of the time she understands when I tell her that she doesn't always get something just because someone else she knows has it. Her sister, on the other hand, wants to know why her friends' houses are bigger than ours, or why she has such a small room compared to theirs. I just smile and tell her it brings us closer together.

I think they are starting to become more comfortable with the belief that life is not about having things, but about having people around you whom you love and who love you back. It is a fundamental lesson from my Sunday school days—"it is easier for a camel to go through the eye of a needle than for a rich man to enter the kingdom of God" (Matthew 19:24).

We all have too much stuff, too much stuff weighing us down, stuff that will surely get caught in the eye of that needle. That's why as parents we need to help our children realize that the path to salvation doesn't require any luggage.

CHLOE: (*Mallory is singing "Amazing Grace" in the background.*) Dear God and Jesus, thank you for letting me read a good book at school. So, so, so good that I screamed. But not in real life. I'm just pretending.

DADDY: You have a new friend—Tina?

CHLOE: Okay, and thank you for getting to have my new friend Tina. She's a new babysitter. And thank you for getting to change the Wii. All you have to do is put a different disc in the Wii.

DADDY: Last thing.

CHLOE: Thank you for my family, and one more thing, thank you for Daddy. Amen.

AMAZING

The backdrop of Mallory singing "Amazing Grace" set the perfect tone for Chloe's prayer on this night. Mallory loves to sing and has a husky, deep, soulful voice worthy of gospel or country music. I could hear her words reverberating off the wall that her room shares with Chloe's room. Fortunately, Chloe didn't seem to be distracted by the *American Idol* audition going on just a few feet from her bed as she said her prayer.

Grif mentioned Chloe's new friend, Tina, on this night because he knows that Chloe is instantly smitten with new people who enter her life. Chloe collects people. Once you meet Chloe and have her attention, she is your friend for life. She loves people who love her, and that's just about everyone with whom she crosses paths. Most of her new encounters end with her hugging the new friend as the person leaves.

"Mommy, I met this girl at dance. I don't know what her name is, but we had *so* much fun," she said one day after dance class, clapping her hands for emphasis. "I can't wait to see her next time."

In many ways it is the glass half full versus the glass half empty metaphor. Chloe loves and trusts you until you give her a reason not to. I, on the other hand have a bad habit of making people earn my love and trust. I honestly think it must be God working through her little heart that allows her to be so open to new people. She brings new meaning to the phrase "Love thy neighbor as thy self."

This is something a lot of grown-ups like myself have not yet mastered. I keep hoping that if I hang out with Chloe and God long enough, some of this will rub off on me.

CHLOE: Dear God and Jesus (*giggling*).

MOMMY: Don't make it silly.

CHLOE: Getting to . . .

MOMMY: Chloe, don't make it silly.

CHLOE: Getting to have playdates with lots and lots and lots of people. I'll tell you their names. Brenna, Nisma, Eden, Taylor. Those are the people I'm going to have playdates with. And Brenna, I'm going to ask my mom if I can have a sleepover with. My first sleepover was with my older friend Michael and his little sister Camryn, that was my first sleepover. And thank you for getting to play out in the rain with our umbrellas with Brooke and Connor. Thank you for my family and one more thing, oh, thank you for Mommy. Amen!

FRIENDS FOREVER

When Chloe was in kindergarten her teacher told me that it took her ten minutes to cross the room to put something in her cubby because she had to stop and speak with everyone in her path. She has a joyful spirit that is unparalleled by anyone else I have ever met. Chloe enjoys playing with the neighborhood children so much that she is always worried about missing something.

"Hurry, Mommy. Help me get my shoes and coat on; the kids are outside! I don't want them to go anywhere without me," she will cry frantically from the front hallway.

"It's okay, honey. They'll wait," I say as I quickly lace her sneakers and then zip up her jacket.

"No, they're faster than me. I have to go *now*," she says, running out the door as I am in mid-zip.

We're fortunate to have several children in our neighborhood with whom she plays on a regular basis. On any given Saturday there is a group of children in and out of our house who engage in an almost 1950s-like freedom in our small cul-de-sac where everyone knows everyone else and looks out for one another's children.

"Getting something," she yells. I hear the door open and the beep-beep-beep sound of the alarm chime. A closet door opens. There is a rummaging sound. Then she appears in the hallway with an armful of stuffed animals and heads back to the front door. "Going out again." This goes on all day long with various combinations of other children trailing her.

Chloe thanks God for her friends in her prayers, and I know she really means it. It makes me think about the friendships I have left unattended because of a busy life and distance; friendships that I want, and need, to rekindle. Even with all the ways to communicate with people these days such as e-mail and social networking sites like Facebook, I feel like I need to reconnect with some of these old friends face-to-face, in a real and meaningful way.

Sometimes it takes a child to help shine God's light on the path that we need to follow.

Chloe on Friends:

Friends are important because if your parents aren't there they will help you. A good friend helps you when you need help. If you get hurt, they will take you to the teacher, or if you forget your lunch they will share some with you.

CHLOE: Dear God and Jesus, thank you for letting me go over to my friend's for a minute when Daddy had to go to band practice and Mommy was at work. And thank you for getting to host a party—me, Brooke, Connor, and Mallory and Alex. There was a disco ball, seriously, there really was. There were balloons. Lots of people came. Miss Dina was the last one. You know Miss Dina's kids always make it fun. We played leap frog with them. And thank you for my family, and one more thing, oh, thank you for Mommy. Amen.

CHASING JOY

Chloe is one of those people who lights up a room. She is an example of the phrase "a party waiting to happen." On this particular day, the girls and their friends had found some leftover balloons and decided to decorate our basement and have their own party. And no one likes a party as much as Chloe. Sure, she loves to dance and eat junk food, but beyond that she loves to spend time with her friends creating joy.

"Mom, what are we going to do for my birthday?" she always says months before the celebration is even a glimmer in the back of my mind.

"I don't know, sweetie. We could go roller-skating or go to the movies with a small group of friends? Something like that?"

"No, Mommy. I want to have a real party!" she always says, and I know exactly what she means. She wants to invite practically everyone she knows.

I am amazed on a daily basis that such a confirmed pessimist created this wholly optimistic child. She is able to find the joy in the tiniest of moments and create joy when there is no obvious joy to be found. That night, after I put her to bed, I wearily cleaned up shards of popped balloons, crushed goldfish crackers, and tiny pieces of glitter that had been spread throughout the entire basement. While on one hand I was overwhelmed by the mess, it also made me realize that maybe we do have to create our own joy, that it isn't necessarily handed to us as a birthright. When I'm with Chloe, I find that it is much easier to experience joy even in the smallest things. Hopefully, with God's love shining through her, she will continue to help me see joy. Once I can see past the pink glitter ground into my carpet, that is.

Tuesday, September 8

CHLOE: Dear God and Jesus, I hope one of my grandmothers, Vi, doesn't die 'cause she's really old, and she's in the hospital. How old is she, Daddy?

DADDY: Sixty-eight.

CHLOE: She's, like, sixty-eight, Daddy said. So she could die pretty soon. And she doesn't want anyone to help at her house, so at nighttime she could have to go to the hospital, and she could be so hurt and tired she couldn't even reach the phone and die. That's sad. And thank you for getting to watch Maximillian's show. And thank you for going fishing with Daddy. And one more thing, oh, thank you for Daddy. Amen.

Love That Skips a Generation

Chloe is particularly concerned when someone is sick. In this case, my husband's mother, Violet ("Vi" for short), has COPD, a pulmonary disease that makes it difficult for her to breathe. She is dependent upon an external oxygen supply. Chloe had obviously overheard more than we knew when it came to conversations about her grandmother's health. There had been many hushed discussions regarding the safety of his mother staying alone in her home two hours away from us.

Chloe didn't seem to really understand that her grandmother had a disease; she thought that she was just sick because she was "old." But her concern about her grandmother being alone in her house, and possibly unable to care for herself, was very real to her even at the tender age of six.

It made me think about how the adults in the family had been looking at it from a purely logistical point of view: Who was going to take care of her? Could they get someone in to help? Would she let them? There was concern in these conversations, but also some rancor, frustration, and feelings of being torn by the different points of view on the subject. Yet Chloe saw it from a purely humanistic point of view. She didn't want something bad to happen to her grand-mother in the middle of the night when no one was there to help her. It made her sad just to think about it.

I wasn't there when Chloe said this prayer, and only heard her words as I went back to transcribe them. She made me see the situation from a different perspective, one that didn't include the consideration of what the adults in the family wanted. I am learning slowly that a child's heart embodies the peace of God that passes all understanding.

CHLOE: Dear God, thank you for learning to ride my bike and play with my friends and going down the big grass hill on my bike and playing with Matthew.

MOMMY: Which grass hill did you go down, the one near Matthew's?

CHLOE: The big, long one.

MOMMY: Near Matthew's house? And you did it? And you didn't fall? I can't believe you learned to ride a bike in a week. And you're so confident.

CHLOE: And thank you for my baby [doll] learning to swim. And thank you for getting to do my Christmas list. And thank you for my family, and one more thing, oh, thank you for Mommy. Amen.

The Humility Train

If I hadn't seen it with my own eyes, I wouldn't have believed it. She was zipping down the street, the purple streamers on the handlebars of her bike flying in the wind behind her. Her pink My Little Pony helmet rode high on the back of her head. The sprigs of blond hair peeked out from beneath her helmet as she gripped the pink handles with fierce determination. Only minutes before this display of bravery, she was sitting on the front porch crying, telling me that she was never going to learn how to ride a bike.

"Mommy, I can't do it," she said with tears in her eyes.

"I know you can, honey. It just takes time. You'll get the hang of it," I replied, feeling helpless to comfort her.

As she watched all the other kids ride in circles around our cul-de-sac, her tears turned to sobs, and she buried her head in her lap. I rubbed her back and comforted her and tried to get her to come inside with me and help me with dinner, but she insisted on staying outside and watching the other kids do something she never imagined she could do.

Minutes later, Mallory came running into the kitchen. "Mommy, come fast. She's doing it. She's riding her bike with no help."

It was as if someone were telling me my baby was walking for the first time. I ran outside, the metal spoon I had been stirring the spaghetti with still in my hand, a dish towel stained with tomato sauce draped over my shoulder. I made it in time to see her cruise by our house and deftly maneuver the sharp turn into our neighbor's driveway. She was even able to lift her death grip on one of the handlebars long enough to give me a small wave.

"You did it!" I yelled, waving the spoon in the air. She rode over to where I was standing and leaned in for a hug as she balanced herself on the bike seat. "I knew you could do it," I said as I tipped her chin up to see her smiling face.

Once she started, there was no stopping her. Thus, her excitement about going down the "big hill" near her friend Matthew's house was a culmination of a week of triumphs on the bike. Yet even when I praised her in the prayer, she simply smiled and shrugged and moved on to another topic. Chloe is not one to brag about her accomplishments. Secretly, inside, I knew she was proud of herself, and it made her feel good that I was proud of her as well. But these two things were enough for her. It was enough for her to know that she had accomplished something with God's help that seemed impossible. And she did it with grace.

The scenario made me wonder about how I might be able to spend more time on humility, focusing less on my accomplishments and more on the accomplishments of others. I think God calls on us to turn our vision outward from ourselves, and when we are truly able to do this, good things happen.

CHLOE: (*singing*) Dear God and Jesus, thank you for playing with my friends and getting to ride my bike without training wheels. Thank you for getting to go to ballet today and getting to practice piano. And thank you for getting to stay with Daddy today and Allison. And thank you for my family, and one more thing, oh, thank you for Mommy. Amen!

POSITIVE ATTITUDE

"I hate doing homework," Mallory said to me one evening when she was tired and had forgotten she had an assignment due the next day.

"Mommy hates a lot of things," I said from a weary place without thinking.

"Like what?" she asked, genuinely curious.

"Like unloading the dishwasher, making lunches, cleaning the kitchen, folding the laundry, making beds," I replied, stopping myself, although I could have gone on and on.

"So, why do you do those things?" Mallory asked.

"Because I have to," I said, wishing I hadn't gotten into such a heavy subject with my ten-year-old at nine o'clock at night.

This prayer made me think about how we can either approach tasks in life with a negative attitude, or we can try to approach them with a positive attitude. Mallory, for example, always complained about practicing piano. It went on for years. The piano practices often ended in tears with Mallory beneath the piano bench, refusing to play, and her father threatening to take away privileges if she did not finish the song.

I remember as a child my parents' halfhearted attempts to get me to play piano. When I refused to practice, they let me quit. To this day, I wish I had stuck with it. Even without natural God-given ability, I might have been able to knock out a few Christmas tunes at a holiday party.

Chloe is now following in her sister's footsteps—initially loving piano, and now starting to resist her father's stringent pleas for her to practice. Her father, Grif, is a musician. He plays piano, trumpet, and drums. One of his biggest desires in life, one with which I totally concur, is passing along his passion for music to his daughters. You see, I can't even carry a tune, and if they've got even one-eleventh of their father's ability, they will easily exceed my musical abilities. It is truly a gift from God, and one that should be nurtured.

"Mommy, do you want to come to my concert?" Chloe asked, dimming the lights in the living room and waiting for Mallory to announce her.

"Of course I do," I said with my arms full of items I had been picking up around the house—a shoe, a Barbie, a newspaper, and an empty water bottle. How could I say no when I should be one of her biggest supporters?

So, on this night, as Chloe thanked God for her piano lesson, I was secretly smiling inside, imagining that her tendency toward having a positive attitude had finally won out over her stubborn resistance. I may not know much about music, but when I sit there watching Chloe's little chubby fingers dance across the keys, her face deep in concentration, the melody floating above the piano, I close my eyes and cherish every moment.

MOMMY: I'm here with one of my favorite people in the whole world, Chloe Griffin, and Chloe's going to do a little prayer for me.

CHLOE: Dear God and Jesus, thank you for getting to do a little dance with my friends Bri and Brooke, and Mallory is my sister, but she started the show. Connor almost did it, but then he went to play with Matthew. Mommy, you know what's weird? I'm thinking . . . Help.

MOMMY: Thank God for the rain that makes the flowers grow.

CHLOE: No. You're ruining it.

MOMMY: I'm going to bed.

CHLOE: Thank you for my family, and one more thing, oh, thank you for Mommy.

Letting Go

On nights when Chloe was distracted and not ready to settle down and pray, I started to *introduce* the prayer as a way to let her know it was time to begin. Sometimes the introductions were sweet, like on this night when I addressed her as "one of my favorite people." Sometimes I simply said, "Take it away, Chloe." I also started trying to set a tone of making this a quiet, reflective time between the two of us and God. In order to make this happen, I would say things like, "This is going to be a quiet prayer."

What I began to realize was that Chloe, even at six years old, was starting to assert her independence with this process. She wanted to be the cruise director of the prayer, and I was only there as her assistant, to throw her a life ring if she should get into deep water.

"I'm too tired to pray," she said to me, her eyes rolling back in her head as she snuggled into her pillow.

"Me too, but I think we should do it anyway," I replied.

"Why?"

"Because it is easy to keep skipping it. I don't think that's what God wants, do you?" I said, rubbing her forehead.

"No. He wants us to talk to him," she said with a tired smile.

Often, she would say "help" in the middle of a prayer looking for me to guide her, but clearly my guidance wasn't always the exact type of help she was looking for. This push and pull of the child-parent relationship reminds me that our jobs as parents are to be guides, to be there, on the sidelines, supporting them, but still allowing them to make mistakes and allowing them to come back and get help when they need it. Ironically, it is similar to our relationship with God. Despite what some people think, I believe God is in a way like a parent, not telling us what to do, but guiding us, allowing us to make mistakes, and encouraging us to come back for help when we need him.

Chloe is perfectly capable of doing a lot of things now. She doesn't need me as much as she used to. But the truth is, just like God, she wants me there in the dark at night, listening to her prayer, my hand ready to reach for hers at a moment's notice. And I will be.

Chloe on Growing Up:

Growing up means there's more room for you to love God and Jesus. Some people want to grow up, and some people don't.

CHLOE: Dear God and Jesus, thank you for getting to go to Mommy's book signing. It was fun and I got to sit next to the table. I never did that before.

MALLORY: You actually sat under the table.

CHLOE: Under the table. It was awesome, awesome. Keep that secret. And I got to play Mallory's Game Boy. Mallory's not awesome right now. (*Mallory is laughing in the background.*) And thank you for letting me have a playdate with Jordan tomorrow. And thank you for . . .

MALLORY: Your big fat nose.

CHLOE: Yours is bigger. Thank you for my family. And one more thing, oh, thank you for Mommy, and Mallory, and Daddy, and my whole family. Amen.

FOR THE LOVE OF OREOS

Both of the girls were wired on this night. Grif suddenly had to go out of town to be with his ailing mother, and I had a book talk at a domestic violence shelter. While Mallory had volunteered with me before at this facility, Chloe knew nothing about the issue, and I wasn't prepared to explain it to her at her age. But I was in a bind. It was a last-minute decision for Grif to go visit his mother, and I had committed to the event months prior. So I opted to wing it and take them with me.

I spoke from a podium and set up my books on a table next to it. The idea was that I would sell my books after the talk and the profits would go to the organization. I set up two chairs for the girls to sit in next to me. Mallory had actually become my little assistant, helping me sell books and make change. But Chloe had never actually been to one of my book signings unaccompanied by another adult to keep an eye on her while I talked. Luckily, the room was small, small enough for me to watch her even as I spoke to the group. Very quickly Chloe honed in on a plate of Oreos on the snack table. I usually reserve treats like cookies for special occasions—holidays, parties, or when we go to a restaurant. I don't buy them at the grocery store or keep them in our house. So, to her, having free reign over a plate of Oreos was like getting to hoard a pirate's treasure.

"Can I have some, Mama?" she asked wide-eyed and hopeful.

"Sure, knock yourself out," I said as I was ticking through my speech in my mind, wondering how I was going to sanitize a talk about domestic violence in front of a six-year-old. Little did I realize that she would never hear a word I said. Instead, she was completely and totally enthralled by the Oreos. *She was under their spell.*

Chloe spent the majority of my presentation under the table of books with her stash of Oreos. Thankfully, she was quiet and allowed me to speak for about thirty minutes and answer questions without interruption. When it was over, I peeked beneath the table and saw her sitting cross-legged with a huge smile on her face. In front of her were fourteen Oreo tops wiped clean of the delectable white frosting, presumably by her little tongue. She grinned at me, and I couldn't help smiling back.

"Mommy, this was so fun. Can I come to all of your book signings?"

"Sweetie, they don't all have Oreos," I said as I scooped what was left of the cookies quickly into my hands before the organizer could see what my child had done.

"Oh, okay, well, just the ones with Oreos," she said, blowing me a kiss and climbing onto the chair, leaving me alone beneath the table. *How did I get here?* I wondered, as I had so many times before in my parenting journey—a grown woman in a dress and heels crouched beneath a table picking up sticky cookie remnants. But then I looked at her little feet in shiny Mary Janes dangling there from the chair near my head and realized that I was exactly where God wanted me to be.

MOMMY: We've had a big day. Chloe is tired, so she's going to do a really quick prayer.

CHLOE: Dear God and Jesus, thank you for going to the movies with my best friends and having a playdate with Jordan and Mallory dressing up funny with her friend Emily. She had a playdate at the same time. And thank you for . . . help me.

MOMMY: How about thank you for pizza for dinner?

CHLOE: Having pizza with the Shermans and watching the movie with Brooke and Connor and the Shermans.

MOMMY: Who are your best friends?

CHLOE: Brooke and Connor.

MOMMY: And thank you for having a half day at school?

CHLOE: Thank you for the half day. Thank you for my family, and one more thing, thank you for Mommy. Amen.

MOVIE MADNESS

When my children were born, I couldn't wait to take them to the movies. I am a movie buff and hoped my children would be too. I'm not a big fan of traditional kids' movies or animation, but I was even willing to suffer through these parental rites of passage in order to get to the other side—PG movies that we could watch together as a family. Don't get me started on the lack of appropriate family-friendly movies that both adults and children can watch without being bombarded with content that makes us cover their little eyes and ears. That's a story for another day.

Chloe's first experience at the movie theater happened when she was about three years old. We had never dared take her sister at this age. But when Chloe was three, Mallory was seven and begging us to take her. So we relented. I don't even remember what the movie was, but I do remember putting our legs up on top of the seats to act as a barrier—Grif on one side and me on the other—to keep Chloe from escaping. Then she got smart and started going underneath our legs. At first she just wanted to sit on the stairs next to our row of seats, which was fine, as long as I could see her. Then she decided to walk in front of the screen. I would see her little blond head bobbing up and down in front of the screen making a tiny shadow as she darted back and forth. Luckily, we were at a children's movie, and no one else in the audience seemed to mind as much as I did. I would try to call her back to her seat in a loud whisper, but inevitably that would cause more disturbance than her big screen debut.

On this particular night we had gone to see *Up* in 3-D. I was surprised that she thanked God for allowing her to go, because she spent a great deal of the movie with her head buried in my lap. While her ability to sit through a movie had improved dramatically, Chloe had never been a big fan of 3-D movies. Her first one was a Hannah Montana movie in which she refused to wear the glasses because she announced, "It makes my head hurt." Of course, with the glasses off she couldn't see a thing and kept screaming that "everything looks fuzzy." Eventually, she became so exhausted by the entire process that she curled up in a fetal position in her seat and went to sleep. The outing was actually for Mallory and some of her classmates from school, so I wasn't that concerned that Chloe decided to opt out of the experience.

I had forgotten just how much Chloe was overwhelmed by 3-D images, and even this cute animated story of a man whose home flies away aided by a bushel of balloons was too intense for her. She gripped my hand fiercely and pulled up the armrests in between our seats so that she could link her arm with mine and lean in to my shoulder. I kept asking her if she wanted to leave, but she assured me she wanted to stay.

"Mommy, is he going to be okay? Promise me he's not going to get hurt," she said, squeezing my hand tightly, waiting for the right answer.

"I promise he is going to be okay," I said, squeezing her hand back. I didn't know for sure, of course, but I assumed. I realized that she felt that with my help, she could get through anything.

I was witnessing the mercy of God's love working through me, making me, of all people, a completely imperfect human being, into a hero to my little girl. Thank you, God.

MOMMY: Take it away, Chloe.

CHLOE: (*In a mock Southern accent.*) Dear God, thank you for picking so many good books, and thank you for getting to ...

MOMMY: Is that supposed to be a Southern accent? It is not a very good one.

CHLOE: I don't know what you're talking about.

MOMMY: It sounds like a Southern accent mixed with a New York accent.

CHLOE: Getting to read good books, riding bikes with my friends, eating candy. And thank you for my family. This is how grandmothers talk. Thank you for my family, and one more thing, thank you for my mommy!

GRITS

My daughters are the product of a mixed marriage—my husband is a Southerner and I'm a Yankee. Ironically, my father was a Yankee, and my mother was a Southerner. So, in a way, history is repeating itself. But while I was raised in the Northeast, my daughters are *girls raised in the South*, better known as G.R.I.T.S.

While Chloe may not have perfected her Southern accent, she has adopted many other aspects of the Southern culture. One of the things I most admire about the South is how the love of God runs as deep in the red clay soil as the roots of an old oak tree. A day doesn't go by when someone won't tell you to have a "blessed day." If you are having a difficult time, Southerners will openly tell you they are "praying for you," and give you a hug to prove it whether they know you or not. And the best part—*they mean it*. In the South faith is like an old familiar robe that you wear year-round no matter how hot it gets.

Chloe fits into this God-culture like the true Southern girl she is. I think it will be easier for her to express her faith here, in a place where open discussions about God are encouraged, than it might be somewhere else. Her ability to express her thoughts about God at an early age has most definitely been shaped by a culture that is open and receptive to people sharing their spirituality.

"God is always there when you need him," Chloe marveled to me one day as she shared her thoughts.

"You're right, Chloe, God is always there—I bet he's also there even when you don't need him. What do you think?" I replied as she nodded in affirmation at my sage tidbit of spiritual wisdom.

I, on the other hand, grew up just outside Philadelphia, Pennsylvania, where discussions and declarations of faith were welcomed only in a solemn setting that involved an altar and a steeple—and even then, *only on Sundays.* But slowly, with Chloe's help, I am becoming more comfortable talking about God and expressing my beliefs.

"Why don't I talk like this?" Chloe says, imitating a Southern twang that sounds like it came straight out of *The Andy Griffith Show.*

"I don't know, sweetie. You just don't," I say.

But what she lacks in her accent, Chloe makes up by being a truly Southern girl through and through—especially when it comes to her unabashed love of God. She is the sum of both parts—the Yankee mother and the Southern father. Yet I know that no matter how many miles she travels from Tobacco Road, she will always be a Carolina girl with a heart full of God.

MOMMY: Should we do our song?

CHLOE: Yes!

MOMMY and CHLOE: (*singing*) She loves me. She gets down on her knees and hugs me. She loves me like a rock, oh baby, she loves me, she loves me, loves me, loves me, loves me. (*kiss*)

MOMMY: Give me a prayer. We're rolling here, fancy pants.

CHLOE: Dear God and Jesus, thank you for getting to get new clothes and underwear. You should have seen it. It's awesome. There's like monkeys on it, like rabbits. It is awesome. I'm wearing a white plain one but the outlinings have pink sparkly stuff. Say hello, Mommy.

MOMMY: Hello, Mommy.

CHLOE: She bought me them. Aren't they beautiful? I love them.

MOMMY: Good. I'm glad. What else are you thankful for today?

CHLOE: Thank you for Mallory getting a big show and doing a show with my friends Brooke and Connor. You should have seen Luke's song. Luke was so cute. Thank you for my family and one more thing, oh, thank you for Mommy. Amen. Bye-bye.

Down on My Knees

Who wouldn't be happy walking around with monkeys and rabbits on their underwear? Maybe adults should try it. Maybe grown-up underwear should be covered with whimsical zebras and hippos. When you're having a bad day, you could just smile to yourself and say in your head, *I may have messed up that report at work, but at least I have panda bears on my underwear.*

In these moments when Chloe is thanking God for things like animals on her underwear, I am humbled into thinking about the small things that I am thankful for—the things that I don't always remember to thank God for. I am thankful for that little square of dark chocolate I snuck when no one was looking after dinner last night. I am thankful for the rain that allowed me to curl up on the couch and write instead of feeling pressure to be outside. I am thankful for the note Chloe left me on my pillow that read: "M=motherly, O=over other mothers, M=mostly nice."

For some reason, as adults it is easy to forget that everything that happens that makes us smile is worthy of a thank-you to God. Children adopt this concept so readily, but it's not as easy for us. So as I watch her effortlessly give God praise for everything from unicorns to underwear, I am transported back to my own childhood when thankfulness came easy, and quite often in these moments I find myself down on my knees.

Chloe on God:

God is like a smile shining down on you. He's like the light going through your heart.

I think he has gray short hair. He wasn't the cleanest man because he's very old. He's been here for a million years, so he's probably not going to quit helping us. He doesn't have any free time. His calendar is already filled up because he has so many ideas.

You just know God is here because he's in your heart, and when you're sad you can feel him.

MOMMY: Here's my beautiful girl to say a quiet prayer.

CHLOE: (*whispering*) Dear God and Jesus, thank you for getting to go to dance today, and thank you for . . . Help me, Mommy . . .

MOMMY: Doing a good job on your homework and your piano.

CHLOE: Doing a good job on my homework and my piano.

MOMMY: The rain for the earth?

CHLOE: The rain. But I didn't like it because I couldn't play outside. And thank you for my family, and one more thing, oh, thank you for Mommy, Daddy, and Sissy. Amen.

Rain, Rain, Go Away

As adults, we learn to censor ourselves, to say what is politically correct and diplomatic, which is not always what we mean. Of course, this is how a civil society operates, but there is something so refreshing about the honesty of a child. In their raw, unfiltered minds, the need for deception or having an agenda is nonexistent.

Chloe and I have spent a lot of time talking about how God is responsible for the earth and all things on the earth. She routinely praises God for the beauty of a rainbow, a sunset, or a perfectly formed wave on a summer day. Usually she finds something positive even in a negative event like an ice storm. She thanks God for having a day off from school, and for having time to play with her friends.

"Thanks, God, for us getting to go sledding all day and stay home from school even though Mommy had to work," she said, shooting me an unhappy glance. "Mommy *always* has to work when it snows."

On this night she wasn't buying my praise for the rain. Adults always feel the need to say things like, "We really needed the rain," whenever it rains, whether we really did or not. Let's face it, unless I'm a farmer or my grass has turned brown, do I ever really want it to rain? Rather than merely accepting my predictable logic that God made it rain to help things grow, Chloe rejected it because the rain had put a damper on her day.

I truly believe in a God who wants us to be honest about our feelings. It's okay to have different opinions. One of the hardest things to do as a parent is to accept that our children don't always share our opinions. I'm sure it's not easy for God either.

CHLOE: Dear God and Jesus, thank you for getting to play with my friends. We haven't played a lot because it's been raining a lot, pouring, pouring, and pouring.

MOMMY: What were your special classes today at school? Anything good?

CHLOE: Going to music and PE and going to church tomorrow.

MOMMY: You're not going to church tomorrow. I just laid your clothes for church early because Mommy is going away tomorrow, and I want to make sure Daddy takes you to church.

CHLOE: Aw, I like church. Help me.

MOMMY: How about just thanks for your friends and your family?

CHLOE: And thank you for my family. (*Mallory is in the room and clears her throat loudly. Chloe turns to address her.*) I usually name anyone who is in the room. I say thank you for blah, blah, blah. Thank you for my family, one more thing, oh, thank you for Mallory, Mommy, and Daddy.

MALLORY: Daddy's not in the room.

CHLOE: And Maggie [the dog]. Wait, is she in the room? Who cares. Amen.

GOD'S HOUSE

Trying to get young children excited about going to church can be about as difficult as getting them to eat broccoli or do math homework. We chose a church before the girls were born and attended it until Chloe was about five. At the time, I was getting a very disconnected feeling that I was just going through the motions. I was going to church because my parents had made me go to church, but I wasn't really getting anything out of it. I also realized that my children weren't getting anything out of it. They fought us every step of the way about going to Sunday school. And even though we had been at the same church for years, we had not established any real relationships with people in the church, nor had my children. I knew this was partially my fault for not making more of an effort. That's when I decided it was time to make a move.

Anyone who has ever changed anything major in their lives knows that change isn't easy. Changing hairdressers, dentists, even grocery stores can be disconcerting. *Where is the mustard? It used to be in aisle two, now I can't find it.* It is easier not to make a change, even when you know it is the right thing to do, and just continue on your familiar course.

I didn't so much do it for me or Grif. I figured we were about as spiritual as we were ever going to be, and that whatever church we went to really didn't matter. Boy, was I wrong. What I didn't realize was that my mediocre approach to faith was being passed along to my children. There was no way I could lead them if I didn't know where I was going.

So we took the plunge. We left our old, solemn, historic downtown church and traded it for a more modern, casual church closer to home— so close that we actually started to get involved in activities other than just the Sunday services. We enrolled Mallory in youth group, and I volunteered for a few different activities at the church. Quickly, people started to know our names at the coffee hour, and our children ran from the service to the Sunday school door without being prodded by us.

"Mom, can I go to the food court?" Chloe will whisper to me during the final hymn of the service. She has taken to referring to the parish hall as "the food court" because our church puts out such a great spread of goodies during the coffee hour. I usually find her double-fisting a cup of lemonade and a cup of cheddar goldfish with a brownie tucked under her arm.

"Yes, but go out quietly," I say as she eagerly climbs over other people to get out of the pew.

These days when I lay Chloe's clothes out for the service, she is excited to go. She took her first communion recently and has even become interested in following along with the service instead of coloring or goofing off.

"Is it time to pray?" she asks me often as she sees everyone kneeling around her.

"Yes, sweetie, it is," I whisper.

"But didn't we just pray a minute ago?" she asks in a loud whisper, prompting smiles from the adults in the pews around us.

"Yes, but we do it more than once," I say in between clenched teeth.

"But I've already said everything I need to say to God," she says.

"Okay, well just close your eyes, bow your head, and try and think of something else to say," I reply, rubbing her back and gently tilting her little head down with my fingertips. I have no doubt Chloe has something else to share with God.

Chloe on Church:

We go to church to show God and Jesus how much we love them, and also to help learn to love them even more. I like sharing the wine and the bread. Listening to the special stories about God. And the food!

MOMMY: We're going to do a quiet prayer tonight because Chloe and I are having some good quiet time.

CHLOE: Thank you for getting to go to Vi's and getting cookies at her place and playing with my friends and getting to see Mommy again, getting a moose from her and a flag. [I was in Canada doing an interview and brought her back a stuffed moose and a Canadian flag.] Thank you for a play-date with Eden, my friend.

MOMMY: And who's coming to visit you Saturday?

CHLOE: And Maddie coming next week. I think about six days, five, I think about five days, and I'm happy about that. Thank you for my family and one more thing, oh, thank you for Mommy. Amen.

Maddie Love

In the week before my mother arrives, Chloe begins to count down exactly how many days it will be before she sees her. Then she wants to know exactly how many days my mother is staying. Chloe and my mother have matching stuffed blue pigs, and when Maddie comes, Chloe always puts hers on Maddie's bed for her to sleep with since Maddie's is back home on her bed in Pennsylvania. Every morning when she gets up, Chloe wants to go downstairs to our little basement guest room and wake my mother up. I always tell her no, but then I turn around, and she is gone.

"I didn't wake her," she says after coming back up the stairs. "I just stood there and looked at her sleeping for a minute. I thought she might wake up, but she just stretched and rolled over."

I picture this scenario, my mother waking up in a dark room to two little eyes staring at her from less than a foot away. Chloe has done this to me before, so I know that it could give someone a heart attack.

"Let her sleep, baby," I say gently. "She'll be up soon."

"But I really, really want her," Chloe says with pleading eyes.

My mom's secret with both of my kids is simply giving them undivided attention. She engages them in a way that a busy parent juggling work and home can forget to do. But grandparents play a different and critical role in the lives of their grandchildren. They are past the frenzy and exhaustion of child rearing, and have a unique ability to concentrate on the things that really matter. To children, attention is love. And to Chloe, there's no better love than Maddie's love.

Observing this love has convinced me of one important thing: I want to be around and involved in the lives of my grandchildren. Right now it seems a lifetime away, but I know that I will close my eyes and in a moment my daughters will be teenagers, then young women, and someday, most likely, wives and mothers.

"What is Mommy going to be when you have babies?" I ask Chloe the question I have asked her so many times before.

"The babysitter!" she says, squealing with delight and clapping her little hands together.

"That's right," I say, closing my eyes, hugging my little girl, and picturing the young woman she will become. I say a silent prayer that God will allow me to be here to see it all.

MOMMY: Take it away, Chloe.

CHLOE: Dear God and Jesus, thank you for going to ballet and getting lots of new shoes and new Crocs. And thank you for getting to eat pizza and chicken nuggets. Thank you for my family and one more thing, oh, thank you for Mommy, Daddy, Sissy, Maggie, and Blue Buddy and Purple Buddy, my entire family. Amen.

THE DEAD FISH

As of this writing, our first fish, Blue Buddy, has been dead for at least three years. Purple Buddy replaced him, and Confetti replaced Purple Buddy. Fish in our house have a life expectancy of about a year if they're lucky. Mallory and Grif started the trend—purchasing the beta fish, *the unkillable fish* according to the pet store manager. They have always lived exactly as the manager instructed—in a bowl by themselves in complete sensory deprivation. No little treasure chest, no plastic seaweed, no little rubber scuba diver man to keep them happy. Just the fish and the bowl. For the most part our fish have always been fed on time, give or take a day or two, and their bowls have always been cleaned in a timely manner. Well, okay, not *always*. There have been moments when I've seen them paddling through murky water trying to get a glimpse of the lamp on one side or the hair brush on the other, anything to break up the monotony. But I'm not the fish person. Grif is. So I tell him that the fish is inhaling his own poop and may die if he doesn't clean the bowl soon. Grif usually rescues the fish just in time.

When I was a child the only kind of fish I had were goldfish won at the church fair. My dad nicknamed them all "Belly-Up" because they died almost immediately after passing the threshold of the Lamb house. But I think for the most part the fish in my adult life have had it pretty good—minus the treasure chest and scuba man, of course.

I'm still amazed that Chloe loves these fish so much that she continues to include them in her prayers even after they are dead. Sometimes the dead fish even rank above family members in her prayers.

"You know what, Mama? Sometimes I just sit and look at Confetti in his bowl and just stare at him. I close my eyes and imagine hugging him. That's how much I love him," she said to me one day. I made a mental note that it was time to get Chloe a pet she can hug. Since our two dogs passed away I had been avoiding adding more responsibility to our household, but Chloe reminded me that it wasn't always about what *I* wanted.

"Mommy, do you think there's a 'pacific fish heaven?'" she asked me one day during a conversation about the deceased fish. "Or maybe there's just like an animal heaven for fish, cats, dogs, all of them. But hopefully we can still visit them."

"I'm pretty sure you can," I said, marveling at how I am always confirming my personal theological constructs as if they are certainties.

If only we could all love as deeply as Chloe loves her fish, living and dead. To be honest, it's not that hard to love; we make it hard. But Chloe has shown me that all God's creatures deserve love, and I can only imagine that there's going to be a big fish tank full of her beloved pets when she gets to heaven.

Chloe on Heaven:

Heaven is like what you mostly like to do—you see a little white spot and that's where you're going. It's like a giant white house. God, Jesus, and people that died already. It's like taking a permanent nap. Nobody ever knows until you go in. You can't come out and tell.

MOMMY: Soft prayer.

CHLOE: Dear God and Jesus, thank you for getting to go to the play area in our church when Mommy went to the meeting. Do you think we will get in?

MOMMY: I think we're going to get in. I like it. I think they like us.

CHLOE: Getting my new books from book order. Playing with baby Ava, Matthew's little baby sister. Thank you for my family. And one more thing. Thank you for Mommy. Amen!

THE CHOSEN ONES

Somewhere in the twenty-first century everything became a contest. Our culture is competition obsessed. From getting a spot in a popular preschool, to getting into a Y-Princess tribe, the world has become a series of hurdles that we must surmount in order to be perceived as the best, brightest, and most powerful. Unwittingly, I must have passed this information along to Chloe because she started to believe at an early age that "getting chosen" was important. When she got a coveted spot in the school her big sister attended, she was thrilled to have been picked. When she visited the school as part of the admissions process, she turned to the teacher unprompted and said, "Thank you. And I would really like to come to your school."

"I didn't tell her to say that," I said to the teacher reflexively as I could feel the redness starting to creep up my face. There was no coaching. Chloe was just telling it like it was.

So it's no wonder that she thought we had to be "chosen" by our new church. I visited first and then started taking the family on a regular basis to see if everyone would like it. It wasn't just about the service; it was about the Sunday school and the people. I wanted to make sure it was a good fit before committing to something so important in our lives.

"Are the people nice?" she asked me after my first solo visit.

"Yes, very nice," I said sincerely.

"But is it fun?" she asked. This was obviously a more complex question since fun to her and fun to me have very different connotations.

"Yes, I think you will think that it's fun."

On this particular day when we attended as a family, I let her and her sister run around the playground after church with some new friends they had met in Sunday school. I was thrilled that they were connecting with other children and having *fun*. I stood at the edge of the playground and chatted with other mothers as we watched our children. I suddenly realized that I was actually having fun as well, something I had not experienced in many years at church, in large part due to my own passivity when it came to connecting with other adults there.

So it took me aback that night when Chloe thought we had "to be chosen" by the church instead of the other way around. But I decided not to dissuade her from the idea because I thought maybe if she thought they chose us, she would feel special and be more excited about going. Turns out I had nothing to worry about. We did choose the church, and in many ways, they also chose us to be part of their community. Not surprisingly, Chloe fits in and feels right at home. I'm on my way. As usual, Chloe and God are leading the way, and I am following.

Sunday, October 4

(*Chloe is having trouble settling down. Mallory is making fun of her.*)

MOMMY: We're not going to do loud prayers. (*to Mallory*) Let her do it.

CHLOE: Dear God and Jesus, thank you for getting to watch videos with my friend and getting to see Mommy's cousin's funeral.

MOMMY: What did you do last night? You did something special last night?

CHLOE: Getting to play with my friends Reese and Riley. Going out with my grandmother shopping, and thank you for getting lots of clothes and a tie dress, that was my favorite one when we went shopping. And thank you for my family and one more thing, oh, thank you for Mommy, Mallory, Daddy, and Maggie. Amen.

This Little Light of Mine

It wasn't my idea to take Chloe to my cousin's funeral. In fact, for most of my life I have been opposed to taking children to funerals. I didn't even attend my grandfather's funeral when I was thirteen. At the time, my mother said she didn't want me to remember him lying in a casket; but instead, she wanted me to remember him smiling at me and embracing me with his large, loving hands. I don't think my mother even looked at her own father in the casket that day.

My husband, on the other hand, believes death is part of life, and that children should not be sheltered from this reality. He has taken both of our daughters to funerals of various distant relatives of his.

But this was the first time *I* had ever taken them to one.

Despite the tragedy of my same-aged cousin's unexpected death, we decided to make the day a time to reconnect with extended family instead of just focusing on the sorrow. We were going to see my mother's relatives in Charlotte, North Carolina. They hadn't seen the girls in a long time, so we decided it was important to bring them. Still, the cause of death had not been determined. So, in addition to it being a sad occasion, there was a tinge of uncertainty about her passing that created another level of stress for the entire family.

But Chloe, being her typical joyful self, rushed right into the group of unknown relatives with a ray of sunshine at her feet. I had lectured her about the solemn nature of the occasion in advance. She listened intently and nodded fervently as I explained that there would be no loud talking or wild behavior. At first, she appeared shy and demure as she greeted everyone, but as soon as she was introduced to my cousin's children, all bets were off. She took to Reese and Riley like they were long lost siblings. At one point, Grif had to take her out of the service because she wanted so badly to talk to them in the pew behind us.

"Reese," she said in a mock whisper that sounded a little bit like it was coming from a bullhorn.

"Chloe, what did we talk about before the service?" I said in a real whisper through a cupped hand over her ear.

At the reception that followed, the adults stood in small groups speaking in hushed tones about my cousin, Martha, drinking punch, and eating cookies and cheese cubes. Chloe and her new friends ran in circles in the grass just outside the reception hall. She had runs in her tights and grass stains on her knees from rolling down the hill next to the church. When it was time to leave she gave me a pout and crossed her arms.

"But I'm having so much fun, Mama. I don't want to leave," she said with tears forming at the corners of her eyes. *Only Chloe could have fun at a funeral*, I thought to myself. I decided that she had the right idea. While the adults concentrated on the darkness of the day, she focused on the light. She reminded me that we all need to spend more time in God's light.

MOMMY: It's Mommy and Daddy's thirteenth anniversary. Tell me what you did for Mommy tonight with Daddy.

CHLOE: Dear God and Jesus, thank you for Mommy and Daddy's anniversary and putting flowers all over and candles all over. It was so pretty. Me and Daddy made it. And going out to Cinelli's and eating a little cake.

MOMMY: Tell me the quote, if I hadn't done what?

CHLOE: If Mommy didn't marry Daddy, then I wouldn't be alive, either would Mallory.

MOMMY: So are you glad that I did?

CHLOE: Yeah.

MOMMY: Do you thank God for that?

CHLOE: Uh-huh.

MOMMY: Anything else?

CHLOE: I've got a good one. At choir there was like a big field of grass with lots of steps. Grass steps, grass steps, grass steps. We sat down there today.

MOMMY: I heard, and you did your homework there?

CHLOE: Yes, we're going to do that every day. Thank you for my family and one more thing, oh, thank you for Mommy. Amen.

The Birds and the Bees

Chloe is the spitting image of her father. To look at us side by side, you would never know she is my daughter. She got zero DNA from me. Friends say they love to get our Christmas card because they have never seen a family in which two children look more completely like one parent. Mallory is my twin.

"Mommy, what did I get from you again?" Chloe always says to me as we look at ourselves in the mirror together.

"We both like to talk," I say, encircling my arms around her neck and kissing her on the top of her head.

"And we have good hearts. It's okay if we don't really look alike."

While Grif and I didn't think it was appropriate to explain the birds and bees to her at such a young age, Chloe knew that somehow Daddy had something to do with making her. It was hard to ignore when everyone was always telling her that she looked exactly like her father.

One day when we were talking about why she so strongly resembled her daddy, she told us she had it all figured out. She said that Daddy had made Mommy a ham sandwich, and that Mommy had eaten the sandwich, and then God put Chloe in Mommy's tummy. Because Mommy ate the special sandwich made by Daddy, God made Chloe look like Daddy. It all inexplicably took place in our cluttered garage.

"That's how it happened," she said with confidence from the backseat of my car. Grif and I stifled a laugh.

"I think that's a very good explanation," I said, squeezing Grif's arm to keep him from dismissing her idea.

On our anniversary Chloe took great joy in helping Grif light candles and spread rose petals around the house. She was so excited when I walked in from work, she could hardly contain herself. Chloe loves seeing other people happy, but on this night it wasn't just about surprising me or making me happy. She takes great comfort in seeing her father make me happy. For children, the love of God is directly translated through the love of their family. If she sees her parents happy, all is right with the world.

"Mommy, you know what I like to hear when I'm going to sleep at night?" she said to me one morning.

"No, sweetie, what?"

"I like to hear you and Daddy talking. I can't hear what you're saying, but I know you are there. It makes me feel safe," she told me.

I pulled her in tight for a hug. She grasped me with both arms around my waist. *Maybe I am doing something right*, I thought in a rare moment of parental confidence. *Amen*, I said to myself in my head. *Amen*.

Chloe on Birth:

I came from my mommy. Someone put me in her tummy, and that would be God. He knew we would be a perfect match. I probably couldn't go with any other family with Daddy's face.

SUNDAY, OCTOBER 11

CHLOE: Dear God and Jesus, thank you for playing with my puppets and going to see Violet. Bringing in my puppets. I haven't seen them in a long time. They're so fun. But I forgot my knight. So I didn't bring him anywhere, because I forgot him. So I used one of my stuffed animals to be a knight, he's a little toy whale. Thank you for Indian Princesses, it was my first day. And thank you for eating Mexican. And thank you for my family, and one more thing, oh, thank you for Mommy. Amen.

MOMMY: That was a great prayer tonight. Good job.

SHOOTING STAR

By the time Grif, a.k.a. "Blowing Horn," started participating in Indian Princesses with Chloe, he was an old pro, having spent three years prior going through the program with Mallory. Technically, for reasons of political correctness, it is now called "Y-Princesses," in reference to the YMCA that sponsors the program, but everyone I know still calls it "Indian Princesses."

This year Blowing Horn stepped up to the plate and decided to start Chloe's tribe. As the organizer, he naturally became the chief of the tribe. Chloe, a.k.a. "Shooting Star," thus became the proud daughter of the chief.

To say watching this display of father-daughter bonding is cute would be an understatement. The goals of the program are to promote the father-daughter relationship, and to encourage children to care about the world around them. Not that Grif needed anything to promote his already close bond with his daughters, but the group became a special way for him to express his love and spend more quality time with his girls.

Whether he is handwriting invitations to the upcoming meeting on seashells or building dream catchers out of popsicle sticks for a group craft, Blowing Horn takes his role very seriously. And Chloe beams at the mere mention of an upcoming get-together with her tribe. She is also keenly aware that her daddy is in charge, and that makes her proud.

"You know, Daddy is the chief," Chloe would tell me proudly every other day.

"Does that mean I have to call him 'Chief'?" I would say jokingly.

"Guess so."

It makes me realize that while our parenting styles are very different—sometimes I get frustrated by his inattention to detail, and he, likewise, gets frustrated by what he perceives as my over-attention to detail—there is an important place for both of us in our daughters' lives.

Anyone who has ever witnessed a sleeping child in her father's arms, her tiny hands wrapped around his neck, her little head nestled in that soft place between his shoulder and chin, knows what it is like to witness the powerful presence of a father's love for a child. I thank God every day that my daughters have Blowing Horn for a father. I can be a lot of things to my daughters, but a father is not one of them.

CHLOE: Dear God and Jesus, thank you for losing my tooth. Not yesterday, not yesterday. Not yesterday. Wait. Not yesterday, not yesterday, but the other day, night. I lost my front tooth. What should I do, Mommy?

MOMMY: I don't know. What did you do today?

CHLOE: Getting to eat mac and cheese and getting to see Allison again. And thank you for my family, and one more thing, oh, thank you for Mommy. Amen.

Dr. Mallory

There was a period of time when my little angel, Chloe, decided to get back at her sister for all the real and perceived wrongs she had done to her by biting her. It happened just a few times, but on two occasions, she lost teeth during the biting incidents.

"Wow, you lost another tooth. That's great," I said to her one night on bended knee as I inspected the spot where the tooth had been. She had given me the news as I walked in the door from work. "You'll have to tell your class during sharing time tomorrow."

"Nope, can't do it," she said, shaking her head vigorously.

"Why?"

"Because it came out when I bit Mallory. I don't think my teacher would like that very much," she said.

The teeth were ready to fall out anyway, but we convinced her that this was not a good plan for losing teeth, nor was it fair to her sister. Luckily, by the time she turned six, she had gotten past this unsavory habit.

Instead, she now turned to her big sister for help with removing her teeth. Being the more squeamish one in the family, the thought of pulling a tooth out of a child's mouth was enough to make me ill. Mallory, on the other hand, had no such impediments to the sight of blood. In fact, she told her dad she thought she might want to be a paramedic when she grows up, so he bought her a first aid kit, and I bought her a requested box of latex gloves. Whenever it was time to pull one of Chloe's teeth out, Dr. Mallory donned her gloves and went to work.

"Come on, Chloe. It's going to be quick," Mallory said. "Open up wide. It will only hurt for a second. I promise."

Chloe looked at her big sister, her eyes wide with apprehension. It was hard for her to accept Mallory in this new role of caregiver after so many years spent having her face smothered with a pillow, doors slammed in her face, and the occasional push or trip in the hallway. Still, Chloe acquiesced and opened her mouth wide for her sister as she sat stoically on the toilet in her pink ballet outfit. Mallory whisked the tooth out with a tissue and then shoved a wad of gauze into Chloe's mouth to control the bleeding. Mallory then ushered Chloe in front of the mirror to look at her handiwork. With tears still dotting the corners of her eyes from the pain, Chloe smiled with her gauze-filled mouth.

As Chloe thanked God for losing a tooth that night, it wasn't just about losing a tooth, or about the Tooth Fairy coming and leaving her a dollar; it was about her big sister saving the day. Once again, God was showing me that there was a divine plan for these sisters to share a lifelong bond, even if a few teeth had to be lost in the process.

CHLOE: Dear God and Jesus, thank you for my massage Mallory gave me and dressing up.

MALLORY: That she's giving you right now.

CHLOE: That she's giving me right now, and for fun she drawed on my back with my mom's makeup, eyeliner. And thank you for getting to read books.

MALLORY: And thank you for Mallory because she's awesome.

CHLOE: Chloe is awesome. Just kidding. And thank you for getting to dance. I used wash cloths. I was dressing up funny. And thank you for my family, one more thing. Okay, Mallory, you know you're going to be in it. Thank you for Mommy, Daddy, and Mallory.

MALLORY: Wait, but I'm last, I want to be first.

CHLOE: Mallory, Daddy, and Mommy.

MOMMY: But I'm last.

CHLOE: Uh, Mallory, Mommy, Daddy.

MOMMY: Okay. Amen.

CHLOE: Amen!

I LOVE YOU MORE

"I love you more," Chloe says many nights as I turn off her light and begin to pull her door closed.

"No, I love you more," I say back to her.

"I love you the most of all," she says, giggling beneath her covers that she has now pulled over her head.

This exchange could and would go on all night if I allowed it to. Sometimes I joke with her about loving her mommy just a little bit more than everyone else, but she always admonishes me on this point.

"Mommy, you know I love *everyone* the same," she says. I half expect her to wink, to show me that she just can't say it out loud, but that she really does love me more.

Recently, when I was sick she gave me a note that she had typed on the computer that said, "I can't wait to see my pretty mother. Sometimes I love her more than the others, shhhhhh." The part about loving me more was in smaller type as if to prove that it was a secret just between us. But in my heart, I know that Chloe loves everyone in her family the same.

The reality is that being anywhere on Chloe's list, just getting a mention in one of her prayers, is a pretty excellent place to be no matter where you rank.

MOMMY: We haven't done prayers in a while. But here's Chloe, take it away.

CHLOE: Dear God and Jesus, getting to do Indian Princesses tonight. And Mommy getting to carve pumpkins with Mallory and me. And thank you for getting tokens because there was a carnival. And thank you for . . .

MOMMY: What did you do last night?

CHLOE: Nothing.

MOMMY: Who was here?

CHLOE: I don't know.

MOMMY: What friend slept over?

CHLOE: Thank you for Cici sleeping over with me.

MOMMY: And who did you play with Friday night?

CHLOE: Nobody. Marshall. My friend Marshall and Wenzori. And thank you for my family, one more thing, oh, thank you for Mommy and my family. Amen.

Best Part of My Day

Mallory is a chip off the old type A block, a child who is happiest when she's constantly engaged in something. But this doesn't work as well for Chloe, who moves at a much slower pace than the rest of us. She needs downtime and breaks in between activities, breaks that I don't always heed.

On this night, Chloe was so weary that her little husky voice could barely form the words to say her prayer. Her eyes were closed as she drowsily repeated the answers I was feeding her. She had had a fun weekend spending time with friends, but she was so tired from all of the activity that she could barely remember what she did.

"Mommy, I need to go to bed," she says to me many nights, tugging on my sleeve as I work on the computer. "I'm sooooooo tired. My eyes are droopy." This immediately prompts strong feelings of guilt in my heart. I get up, scoop her up, and take her to her room.

Chloe is the type of person who will run in circles as long as there is room to run, but as soon as someone stops her, and she is inactive for a moment, she will fall asleep on the spot. She is so afraid of missing something that she tries to keep up, especially with her big sister. As her mother, I need to be more cognizant of her need for downtime and try not to fill her every waking moment. I've actually learned that Chloe's pace is a nice change for me. As I write this, she is sitting in front of the fireplace watching a cartoon and coloring a homemade snowflake that we made together after playing several alphabet word games. On her head is a crown she has fashioned out of a Styrofoam cup and a piece of yarn. I, too, have a matching crown that she made for me. If people could only see me now. All is right with the world. Whenever I allow myself the luxury of just being with my children with no plan or agenda, I discover the best part of my day. Without all the noise that normally clouds my busy life, I am finally able to find the best parts of myself, thanks to Chloe and the subtle orchestration from God.

CHLOE: Dear God and Jesus, thank you for making a Halloween party with lots of games like with a bean bag toss, you throw bean bags and there's like two eyes and a mouth, you try to throw them in the holes of them and the eyes are worth five points and Miss Schnurr got fifteen on her first time. You go three times and then you got to go to the back of the line.

MOMMY: Anything else?

CHLOE: There's a bingo thing with monster faces. You got all of them you would win and you could get a pencil.

MOMMY: Did Mommy do anything at the party?

CHLOE: Mommy came to make arts and crafts. There were these pumpkins, you get to decorate them with houses and scary trees, bats and ghosts and a moon.

MOMMY: And what else?

CHLOE: And there was fruit snacks. I think that's all the games.

MOMMY: Did anybody read?

CHLOE: Thank you for Mommy reading the book. What other games did we do? The pumpkins, the bingo.

MOMMY: Did we have a playdate today?

CHLOE: Thank you for having a playdate with Nisma.

MOMMY: And what do you have tomorrow?

CHLOE: Having a playdate with Brenna. I already knew that.

MOMMY: Anything else, want to thank God for your family?

CHLOE: I'm thinking. Thank you for my family, one more thing, thank you for Mommy, Daddy, and Sissy. Amen.

GETTING CREDIT

When you're a working mother, you want to get credit for every volunteer effort you make at your child's school, because it doesn't happen on a regular basis. If you help out in the classroom or drive on a field trip, it usually means jumping through hoops to get time off from work. So you want to make sure your effort doesn't go unnoticed by your child who seems to notice everything the other mothers do, but not always what *you* do.

"Mommy, how come you don't read to the class on Wednesdays? And how come you don't ever come to game day?" Chloe asks me routinely even though she already knows the answers to her questions.

"Sweetie, Mommy works on Wednesdays and on game day. I do what I can," I say, hoping that someday she will understand.

How can you explain to a six-year-old that the television news is on every day at five o'clock in the afternoon, and the times to volunteer in the classroom are directly at odds with a murder trial, a hostage situation, or a raging brush fire? It is a job unlike other jobs where flexibility is an option. In television news there is no flexibility. Once you are on the clock you are owned by the news until you are released when the job is finally done, and that's rarely at a specific time that you can plan your schedule around.

On this day, I was a little too determined to make sure she realized her uncrafty mother led the arts and crafts segment of her Halloween party. I am in awe of mothers who snap their fingers and come up with an engaging and non-messy craft, or who can whip up healthy, creative snacks on a moment's notice for a class function. I am not that person. For me, these tasks require a great deal of planning and effort.

For the Halloween party I brought stick-on foam shapes to decorate the foam pumpkins with. I also brought gems and glitter glue. I didn't anticipate the time required for glitter glue to dry, nor did I take into account the cleanup required after all those little papers came off the backs of the foam shapes, but overall the kids seemed to enjoy the project.

I knew Chloe appreciated my being there and was proud that I got to read a Halloween story to the class, one area in which I actually feel confident when it comes to entertaining children. I think in her own way she understands that I am busy, and that, when I make the effort to be involved, I try to go all out. Truthfully, she doesn't really compare me to other mothers the way I compare myself to them. She is just happy that I'm there, and I thank God for that.

CHLOE: Dear God and Jesus, thank you for getting to go to church today and play with my friends.

MOMMY: Think about the whole weekend because we didn't say a prayer last night.

CHLOE: And Maddie coming for Halloween, and yesterday being Halloween and thank you for . . . Help, help me . . .

MOMMY: What did you do Friday night? You had special time with a friend Friday night?

CHLOE: Playing with Cici on Halloween.

MOMMY: And Friday night you had another friend, Liz.

CHLOE: Playing with my friends Katherine and Elizabeth.

MOMMY: How about just wrap it up? I think that's good.

CHLOE: Thank you for my family. And one more thing, oh, thank you for Mommy, Maddie, Sissy, and Daddy. Amen!

MOMMY: She is a prayer warrior.

PRAYER WARRIOR

Eventually no matter how tired Chloe was, our bedtime prayer became a ritual that she didn't want to skip, despite her earlier assertions to the contrary. Oftentimes my work schedule meant the bedtime ritual started later than I would have liked, but nonetheless, I decided it was still important, and so did she. Not only was it a calm moment that helped her fall asleep just before bed, but it was a rare, quiet, peaceful time for us to share at the end of another chaotic day. Now, on some rare occasions when I travel for work, we even say prayers together over the phone.

Chloe's biggest concern was always missing something in the prayer. If she missed something, she always wanted a do-over. I told her that was not necessary, that God would understand and she could simply add whatever she felt like she had missed at the end of the prayer. Under protest, she would do this. I told her that God didn't keep score of what she thanked him for and what she forgot, that he was just happy she was talking to him.

"Mommy, I forgot about the ice cream," she would say with a voice bordering on hysterical.

"No worries, sweetie, he knows you're thankful for the ice cream," I would reply gently.

As usual, we had had a very full weekend including Halloween festivities. Chloe dressed up as Dorothy from *The Wizard of Oz*, and Mallory was Hannah Montana from the Disney Channel. My mother, who loves to see the girls dress up, was visiting, and she and I decided to be witches. My mother's ensemble was a glamorous witch costume ordered from a fancy catalog; mine was a Target T-shirt that read "Good Witch" and a cape, hat, and broom from the girls' dress-up box.

"Mommy, Maddie's costume is much better," Chloe said, assessing the two of us as we posed for a picture together.

"I know," I said between gritted teeth as I tried to smile for the camera. "It's the best I could do on short notice."

Chloe especially loves fantasy, so Halloween is one of her very favorite holidays. In her blue and white gingham dress, with her red ruby slippers, pigtails, and her stuffed Toto in a basket, she looked every bit of Dorothy. She was a sharp contrast to Mallory in her blond Hannah Montana wig with her rock-and-roll minidress and pink Converse sneakers. But despite their contrasting costumes, their joy was equally shared as they ran around the neighborhood with their friends, going door-to-door while the parents followed at a prudent distance with flashlights and backup candy bags.

"Mommy, look how much I got," Chloe would say periodically, opening her bag to show me under the glow of a streetlight. "I can barely carry it." That was code for, *Mommy, in a minute you're going to have to carry it for me.*

After all the hoopla, and the inevitable crash from the candy high—we had no prayer on Halloween—we had to get back on the horse the next night. But despite her weariness, my prayer warrior soldiered on and ended her day in the same way she now ends all her days—thanking God for her many blessings. It made me think of all the times I'm too tired to thank God for my blessings, and made me realize that's exactly when I need to do it.

Chloe on Prayer:

It's important to pray because maybe your friend got hurt and your friend had to go to the emergency room and it might be a miracle, and they might get better. It usually happens when you pray a lot—miracles usually happen when you pray a lot.

It makes me feel like I'm helping someone, or I'm telling God a story, telling someone's story.

You have to thank him because he pretty much controls if miracles happen or not.

CHLOE: Dear God and Jesus, thank you for Maddie coming, reading a really good book, *I Love My White Shoes*. It has a song and it's a book, and thank you for getting to . . . Help . . .

MOMMY: What did you do today, anything fun?

CHLOE: Maddie gave me this new sketch book. (*She is sketching in it as we talk.*)

MOMMY: Ooh. That's a thing to be thankful for.

CHLOE: 'Cause I love it.

MOMMY: Anything else?

CHLOE: Help.

MOMMY: Playing piano with Daddy?

CHLOE: Getting to play piano with Daddy. Having dinner with Mallory.

MOMMY: How about thank you for my family?

CHLOE: Thank you for playing with my friends this week, and thank you for my family, one more thing, oh, thank you for Mommy, Daddy, Maddie, Sissy. Amen.

MOMMY: That's a good prayer.

SEEING THE SHADOWS

From a very young age Chloe has said she wants to be an artist—much like a child says he or she wants to be a firefighter, police officer, astronaut, or ballerina. Unlike some childhood fantasies, I believe that art will play a big role in Chloe's future. She has always loved drawing, but more than that she loves *creating*. This is the one area where I can finally see my daughter's DNA intertwined with my own. When I was a child, my grandfather in North Carolina would give me cardboard boxes, scissors, and magic markers, and I would spend hours creating little towns, fashioning buildings out of the boxes and paper dolls out of the box lids on his screened-in porch.

"Are you going to use that?" Chloe asks me every time I try to discard a cardboard tube from an empty roll of toilet paper or paper towels.

"Nope, you can have it," I say, handing it over to her reluctantly. I know that I will eventually find it hanging from a piece of yarn somewhere with pieces of crepe paper attached to it, and possibly another one of her colorful "art projects" stuffed inside.

Chloe's absolute favorite things to create for some inexplicable reason are outfits out of tissue paper for her stuffed animals and Barbies. I constantly find little stuffed bears and rabbits wrapped in toilet paper sarongs with little toilet paper hats taped to their heads, and Barbies with crudely fashioned off-the-shoulder evening dresses. While finding little bits and pieces of her discarded tissue paper around the house drives me crazy, I have to admit that I admire her creativity.

"Mommy, to be a good artist you have to be very still and be able to see the shadows," she told me recently.

So I was not bothered that she was using her new sketch book as we prayed on this night. She was clearly thankful for her grandmother's gift. And I was thankful for God's gift to Chloe that allowed her to see the world through the eyes of an artist.

CHLOE: Dear God and Jesus, thank you for Mallory giving me some books she wrote, reading really, really good books when I read. Mommy read one page, because it was really, really hard, because it took me eight minutes to finish it. It's really short. And thank you for eating a really good dinner, egg noodles, they're really good. You should try them again. Thank you for putting out the deer corn, and today we saw deer, and going to dance, and thank you for . . . Help . . .

MOMMY: Your family.

CHLOE: And when Maddie leaves to Pennsylvania, whatever it's called, Philadelphia, she's not going to be away from us, because we're going with her. Mommy, I want Daddy to come.

MOMMY: I know, sweetie, but Daddy can't. He's got to work.

CHLOE: But you take days off.

MOMMY: I know, but I'm a mommy.

CHLOE: Thank you for my family, and one more thing, oh, thank you for Mommy.

MOMMY WARS

Being a working mother is probably one of the biggest challenges I have ever faced in my life. When I work, I miss things with my children. Because I work, there are some activities in which they cannot participate because I can't work out the transportation. I have an all-or-nothing job. When I am at work, I have no idea where I will be that day or when I will be done. I can be sent two hours away, and I am always in a news car with someone else driving, which means I have little control of my schedule. When everyone else's workday is winding down late in the afternoon, mine is heating up as the newscasts approach.

In addition to my television job, I also work on my writing projects at night after the kids have gone to bed. I call this my "third shift"; taking care of my family and home comprise my "second shift."

There is also guilt when I am home with my family or at a book signing and my office calls and needs help and I have to tell them I'm not available. But at the end of the day, I know the most important job I have is being a mother. It is also the one job that I can't do over if I fail; and if I fail, the consequences are much more serious than if I screw up at work. So I am the one who takes more days off, some paid, some unpaid, to be with my children over holiday breaks and during teacher workdays.

"You're off today!" Chloe says sleepily as she looks up from her pillow and sees that I am in workout clothes instead of a business suit. "Yay," she says in a husky voice.

Despite the intensity of my jobs and the amount of effort I put into them, Grif's job actually supports our family for the most part. So he is the one who works when the kids are out of school, and I am the one who usually takes care of them. He does pull the occasional snow day or sick day. But explaining to children why a parent can't go with them on a trip or why Mommy can't come to the Valentine's Day party at school is never easy.

"I want to be there, sweetie, but it's in the middle of the day. I don't have any idea where I'll be at that time," I tell her, wishing all school functions parents were asked to attend were first thing in the morning.

The "Mommy Wars," as they've been dubbed, refers to the debate between working mothers and stay-at-home mothers. But in reality, I think the mommy wars are really between a mother and her own expectations of herself. I want to be the best mother I can be, but I also want to be a good television reporter and a good writer. Can I do it all? Should I even try? What is "enough" when it comes to having a full life and being proud of what we have accomplished? *God, family, work*. I know the hierarchy, but sometimes the lines get blurred.

As I sit here with my little tired angel, thinking about her wide-eyed and jumping up and down as she watched the deer in our yard earlier in the day, or thinking about how she is trying so hard to learn to read "big-girl books," I know that God has truly blessed me. I just need to learn to trust what I already know in my heart. Without saying anything, Chloe and God let me know that being a mother *is* enough.

CHLOE: Dear God and Jesus, thank you for getting to go roller-skating and getting my flu shot quickly over today, which I hate. It actually didn't feel that bad. I holded Sally tight and I didn't even look at her. I had it, and I didn't really feel anything. It was sore when I went out. It hurt so bad, because it was sore.

MOMMY: Did you get a sticker?

CHLOE: I got an Ariel sticker, but I lost it in Daddy's car. Thank you for going roller-skating with Indian Princesses. Thank you for my family, and one more thing, oh, thank you for Mommy. (*kissing sounds*) We have to remember that, you have to press it and then do it.

MOMMY: The kissing hand.

CHLOE: Yeah.

MOMMY: You have to press it.

The Kissing Hand

Not being with your children during important moments in their lives is one of the most difficult things about being a working parent. This particular year the swine flu had become an epidemic. The vaccine was almost impossible to get. People stood in line for hours at the health department to get their children vaccinated from the limited supply. I was not able to take a day off from work to do this, but when I found out my doctor's office had recently gotten in a small shipment, I jumped at the opportunity to get my children the shots.

Thankfully, a friend from work who sometimes babysits my girls, Sally, agreed to take them to the appointment. I don't like taking my own children to get shots; I've had to pull Chloe out crying from beneath the exam table on more than one occasion. So taking another person's children to get flu shots qualifies you for sainthood in my book.

"I have to get *a shot?*" Chloe asked me with tears welling up in her eyes. I decided not to tell her until the day of the appointment. I'm still not sure this was the best tactic.

"Sweetie, yes. Mommy doesn't want you to get sick. It's important. I know you're scared, but it's just something we have to do," I said, pulling her in tightly for a hug as crocodile tears began to roll down her little cheeks.

When I'm not with Chloe during these important moments, we came up with a way for her to *feel* as though I am with her. It comes from the book *The Kissing Hand* by Audrey Penn. In the story the mother raccoon and her child, Chester, kiss each other's paws and then press them to their faces to feel the warmth of the other one's kiss when they are apart. Somehow, I convinced Chloe that it really worked, and we started doing it on a regular basis.

"Mommy, you have to kiss it real hard or it won't work," she instructs me when we perform this ritual. Sometimes I kiss her hand multiple times for emphasis. After that, she kisses my hand, and I put it to my cheek to pretend like I am checking out the effectiveness of her kiss.

"Nope, not strong enough, need more kisses," I say, holding my hand up to her as she giggles and gives in to my request.

What I didn't know is that the kissing hand works both ways. Recently, I was having a bad day at work, and I remembered that Chloe had kissed my hand that morning. I sat at my desk with chaos all around me and closed my eyes, pressing my palm to my cheek. In that instance I became a believer. All the bad stuff disappeared, albeit for a moment, and I felt the warmth of my daughter's love. In my world that qualifies as a miracle, and we all know who is in charge of those.

3

HAPPY BIRTHDAY, BABY JESUS

Remember, if Christmas isn't found in your heart, you won't find it under a tree.

—CHARLOTTE CARPENTER

CHLOE: Dear God and Jesus, thank you for getting all our Christmas stuff out, but we didn't get a Christmas tree, but everything else like our books and other things, decorations I play with. There's like these Jesus stables. There's one I really like. And thank you for Merry Christmas books. [We have a tradition of getting the Christmas decorations out early, in increments, so we can enjoy the season as long as possible.]

DADDY: Chloe, you hear the big news? We may be going to Camp Kanata this weekend with Indian Princesses.

CHLOE: Like spend the day?

DADDY: I worked out a special day just for you.

CHLOE: Just to spend the day?

DADDY: No, they have an outing.

CHLOE: Like a sleepover?

MOMMY: To do all the stuff you missed last Sunday, and you get to do it with Cari Beth. Go on the hike, have a campfire with Cari Beth. What else do you want to thank God for? Let's finish up, baby. I'm sorry. I'm tired.

CHLOE: Thank you for . . . Now you made me forget it.

MOMMY: I'm sorry.

CHLOE: A book that we read. I picked it out. Thank you for my family, and one more thing, oh, thank you for Mommy, Daddy, Sissy. Amen.

The Jesus House

Eventually, Chloe graduated from loving Baby Jesus to loving the entire manger scene. My mom gave her a pretty porcelain set that she proudly displayed in her bedroom. I had also purchased a cheaper version from Walmart that had real straw adorning the barn. I realized this was a bad idea when I came home and found the straw spread all over the house.

"Mommy, please get my Jesus houses down," Chloe says from the bottom step of our pull-down attic every year. She is far more interested in the manger scenes than the Christmas tree. They provide her with endless hours of entertainment in the weeks leading up to Christmas.

One day I started noticing that the characters were missing from the cheaper version of the Jesus House when I returned home from work at night.

"Where are Joseph, Mary, the wise men, the animals?" I asked Chloe with my hands firmly placed on my hips that were cocked at a sharp angle to prove that I meant business. I was annoyed at constantly having to do a search-and-rescue mission for the holy team.

"Having a party," she said nonchalantly as she took my hand and led me back to her bedroom. There I saw two Josephs, two Marys, six wise men, two Baby Jesuses—you get the picture. The fancy porcelain ones were side by side with the cheaper versions whose paint was already wearing off, making them look like weary knockoffs of their more expensive twins.

"So, why did you decide to combine them?" I asked, dropping to my knees to hug her, knowing the answer was going to be good.

"Because it is Christmas. It's about being together, right?"

CHLOE: Dear God and Jesus, thanks for getting to read *Amelia Bedelia* and thank you for getting to . . . Help . . .

MOMMY: What did you do today? Piano?

CHLOE: Piano. Getting to start a new book. Not a new book, a Christmas book. And thank you for the dads having a spaghetti lunch starting November 20. How many more days is that?

MOMMY: It's awhile.

CHLOE: And thank you for going to Camp Kanata on Sunday.

MOMMY: What are you drawing?

CHLOE: Me.

MOMMY: You're drawing you?

CHLOE: Jordan is good at drawing like this, so I just copied how she did it with the neck. Look how good the hand is. I cannot draw that good. It is bad.

MOMMY: You are a good drawer.

CHLOE: And thank you for my family, and one more thing, oh, thank you for Mommy. Amen!

Following

Unlike most adults, kids have a tendency to learn from one another. Rather than coveting another person's skills, a child is able to take the opportunity to really learn something from a friend. Chloe has always loved art, but in the beginning of her drawing life, she drew stick figures that amounted to a head with arms and legs. The body of the person was usually missing.

"Not very good, Mommy," she would say, assessing her work out loud.

"No, sweetie, I think it is good. I know it is a person," I'd reply, not knowing how delicately I needed to tread.

"You think everything I do is good because you're my mommy," she would say with an ear-to-ear grin.

"True, baby, very true," I'd say as I was caught by a six-year-old in the oldest parenting trick in the book—praising everything, even when it's not perfect.

But the truth is that Chloe's drawing has greatly improved, in large part due to the fact that she has watched her friends, like Jordan, and learned from them.

"Jordan draws great bodies," Chloe told me one day. Soon, bodies started to appear in Chloe's drawings.

I am so proud of her, not just because she is a good little artist, but mostly because she is not afraid to try things and to borrow techniques from others when she is learning a new skill. It is something adults could benefit from if we would only allow ourselves to be humble enough to admit that other people sometimes do things better than we do. It's something I am working on. God can give us all the talent in the world, but without perseverance and humility, there's a good chance it will amount to nothing.

CHLOE: Dear God and Jesus, thank you for going to our friend Owen's, and thank you for . . . Help . . .

MOMMY: Playing with your friends today, working on the Christmas tree.

CHLOE: Going rock climbing and working on the Christmas tree. (*crying*)

MOMMY: What's wrong?

CHLOE: That thing.

MOMMY: The thing that broke? It's okay, sweetie, we've got plenty more ornaments.

CHLOE: I didn't put it up. That's the ornament Santa Claus brang.

MOMMY: Honey, we'll get another Santa Claus ornament. It was an accident. It's no big deal.

CHLOE: Thank you for my family, and one more thing, oh, thank you for Mommy and Daddy. Amen.

Spilled Milk

Chloe has always been a very sensitive child. When she does something wrong, or even perceives that she has done something wrong, she usually runs crying to her room. I then go and try and comfort her, coax her through the door to come out. Unfortunately, she doesn't always buy my sincere pleas that I'm not upset with her—especially when whatever she has done is an accident (and it usually is). I'm also not a person who invests a lot of importance in things. Things can be replaced, and I want my children to know that. It's like that old expression "Don't cry over spilled milk."

On this night as we were unwrapping Christmas ornaments that had been wrapped in newspaper and stored for a year in our attic, Chloe accidentally dropped an ornament shaped like Santa Claus. It fell on the hardwood floor in our den and shattered into a hundred tiny pieces. She looked down in horror at what had happened. Because I knew how she was feeling, I tried to tell her right away that it was just an accident, not something she needed to be worried about. It was a pretty ornament, but not one with any special significance. In fact, I couldn't even recall where we had gotten it. Still, Chloe would not listen to my insistence that she had done nothing wrong. Even hours later during her prayer she was still dwelling on the issue.

"Mommy, I ruined *everything*," she said in between sobs.

"Honey, no you didn't. You didn't ruin anything. We had a great time putting up the ornaments. The tree looks beautiful. *You* made it look beautiful," I said, trying to comfort her.

I think God has given Chloe a heart that feels deeply about everything and everyone around her. When she thinks she has hurt someone either directly or indirectly, it hurts her heart. I am so humbled to have a child like this. As adults who frequently move at the speed of light—too fast sometimes to recognize the needs of others—humility and compassion are often missing in our lives on a daily basis. Through the innocence of a child's heart God helps us see that we can do better, and at the same time, we can also help our children learn not to cry over spilled milk.

MOMMY: Chloe's had a really big day.

CHLOE: Dear God and Jesus, thank you for getting to go to Camp Kanata. There was rock climbing. There was a little rope you can hang on. You earn something like a badge, like a badge. Thank you for letting me play with my friends today. Thank you for my family and one more thing, oh, thank you for Mommy. Amen.

WET BADGE OF COURAGE

Getting a badge in Y-Princesses is a big deal for Chloe. She works hard for her accomplishments. In many ways, she reminds me of myself. I have always had more tenacity than natural-born talent, and it has served me well. On swim team, Chloe was always placed in a heat that didn't affect the overall score of the event. Only the first heat of every stroke actually counts toward the total. But we never told her that. We just wanted her to have fun, get some exercise, and feel like she was improving a little bit each time she got in the water.

One particular night, she was in the third heat for the backstroke. I had come straight from work and was volunteering, which involved lining up all of the first graders in the right order for each heat. Not only was I in high heels, but I didn't know most of the children's names, so I was at a distinct disadvantage.

"Mommy, she's winning," Mallory said excitedly as she tugged on my arm, jumping up and down, spraying drops of water from her wet hair all over me like a dog shaking after a bath. I pushed through the crowd to the edge of the pool and saw my baby with a huge smile on her face gliding through the water on her back. She got hung up for a second on the rope on the side of the lane, and I thought it was over.

But the next thing I knew, she was back on track. When her little blue fingertips hit the wall backward, I reached down and pulled her up out of the water.

"You won!" I said, surprising both of us. She had never won anything before, especially not anything that involved athleticism. She smiled and we hugged. I didn't mind that her wet bathing suit soaked my business suit. A woman handed us a first-place ribbon over my shoulder, and I handed it to Chloe. She looked at it and grinned again.

"Mommy, will you hold on to this for me?" she said, beaming. "It's special, just like my Indian Princess badges."

"It sure is, sweetie, it sure is," I said, looking down at my "badge" of parenting—a wet suit and a full heart.

(Mallory is with us in Chloe's room.)

CHLOE: Dear God and Jesus, thank you for getting to . . .
  Help . . .
MOMMY: What did you do today?
CHLOE: Nothing.
MOMMY: You did nothing?
CHLOE: Except for go to school.
MOMMY: Was there anything good at school?
CHLOE: We went in the little woods like on the side of all the
  trees that goes back. We walked to at the end, where we're
  allowed to go. We're not allowed to go there actually.

  Thank you for getting to see my friends and his big sisters and, there was, like, when the parents were downstairs,
  they videoed the whole thing and they could see us on their
  TV. I know how to spell TV. T-dot-V-dot. Thank you for
  my family and one more thing, oh, thank you for Mommy,
  Daddy, Sissy, and Maggie.
CHLOE, MOMMY, and MALLORY: *(singing)* Amen.

Coloring Outside the Lines

It is important to point out that even though Chloe has the heart of
an angel, there are times when she's no angel. She likes to push the
envelope. While her sister is generally a rules girl, Chloe likes to see
how far she can stretch boundaries.

As a very young child, hiding was Chloe's specialty. One time she
was behind a chair in our living room while neighbors searched the
dark woods behind our home for an hour with flashlights until a friend

found her crouched in the corner. Another time she hid under the bed at my mother-in-law's house on Christmas while my husband's family canvassed people up and down the street looking for her. On more than one occasion (most recently at Disney's Animal Kingdom), I have lost her for a few moments as she wandered away distracted by something. This of course sends me into a total body panic attack that usually leads to screaming hysterics until I finally locate her (at Disney for example, she was looking at some monkeys swinging from a nearby tree).

"Mommy, I was right here the whole time," she said to me as I hugged her and cried in front of the monkey exhibit. "It's okay," she said, gently stroking my back.

"But you scared Mommy to death. Promise me you will never do that again," I said as I pulled back, trying to give her my sternest look that I could muster through welling tears.

So it was no surprise to me that she had pushed the limits of where she was allowed to walk on her playground at school. And, honestly, instead of getting mad, I try and understand that creative children will always color outside the lines.

I am a rules girl. What I have learned from Chloe is that sometimes our curiosity and creativity lead us to places that are outside the lines, places where it is okay to bend the rules a little. At the same time, I try to instill in her that safety is a priority, and that she needs to be mindful of *which* rules are very important to follow.

The bottom line—Chloe's no angel, and neither is her mother. But with God's grace we keep it inside the lines most of the time.

MOMMY: She had a really big day and she's going to tell you about it.

CHLOE: Dear God and Jesus, thank you for getting to go to Jordan Lake. We had paper, like, five pieces, and it was, like, yellow, red, orange, brown. What did you see that was yellow? What did you see that was red and stuff? And you write a sentence about it. This other sheet was you're supposed to sit somewhere and sketch something, and I sketched the pond. There was another one, you sat under a tree and what did you hear? One was what animals did you see?

MALLORY: Did you see any animals?

CHLOE: Daddy longlegs.

MALLORY: That's not technically an animal, but go on.

CHLOE: And there were games. He had this toy saw. We standed somewhere and trees can't move so we just sat in one spot. Then once he tapped your shoulder with the saw, there was people holding up signs, pretend it was like pine and woodpecker and strawberry, pretend those are real. So it was like he would tap on your shoulder and say "strawberry." You would go behind that person that had the sign with strawberry. And this other one was trees cannot move right. So what we did was, he sprinkled little cards like yellow, blue, and red. So it's like the blue stands for water, the yellow stands for sun, and something stands for red. You try to get each one of those colors, when he says go, you try to grab all them you can, but you cannot move your feet.

MOMMY: Wow, that's quite a game.

CHLOE: It was really fun. You would get it if you saw it. And thank you for getting to read a really good book. Getting to go in Taylor's car and watching *The Three Musketeers*. We watched it in Taylor's car. Thank you for my family, and one more thing, oh, thank you for Mommy, Mallory, Daddy, wait, yeah, and Maggie and Maddie and Pop Pop. Amen!

Daddy Longlegs

My daughters' school places a big emphasis on the environment and our role in protecting it. I have to admit that this has never been a strong point of mine, but I'm getting better. I am a dedicated recycler, but I still use too many plastic bags according to my kids and sometimes let the water run when I brush my teeth.

"Mommy, you're wasting water," Chloe screams as she edges in between me and the sink and turns off the faucet as I am in mid-brush.

"I'm going to be quick. I just left it running for a second," I say with garbled words through a mouthful of toothpaste.

"God does not like it when you waste his water," Chloe says to me with complete sincerity.

I could just picture her sitting beneath that tree at the park on the field trip listening and looking for God's creatures all around her. The fact that she saw a daddy longlegs, which are almost impossible to see against the backdrop of pine straw, leaves, and brown grass, is also typical of Chloe. She is keenly aware of the world around her— and in the stillness, beneath that tree, she was even more able to take in every tiny detail.

I need to try and find a way to have that same stillness in my life so that I can be aware of everything around me instead of just seeing things pass by me in a blur as I race from one thing to another. Sometimes I think that's why God gives us children. So that we, too, might someday be able to see the daddy longlegs.

MOMMY: I've got Chloe Griffin the ladybug here, and she's going to do a nice, sweet prayer.

CHLOE: Dear God and Jesus, thank you for getting a new ladybug hat. It was so cool. I will take a picture of it and put it in our prayer book. Mom, we gotta take a picture of it. Don't tell anyone.

MOMMY: Okay.

CHLOE: And for Mallory making a cool thing. It's like in a cardboard box. They took a piece of paper and made it orange as a nest and made, like, two white balls out of clay, and made like an eagle out of clay, and it's like she cut out a sign and put green paper for the grass and blue paper for the sky, and she put, like, clouds hanging down with paper, and there were words you could read. Information about the eagle and stuff. Thank you for . . .

MOMMY: What did you do today?

CHLOE: Having no school today, having piano.

MOMMY: Didn't you have a playdate today?

CHLOE: Having a playdate with Taylor. Guess what? Guess what? Guess what?

MOMMY: What?

CHLOE: So we put yogurt all over our face, and we ate half a grape and put it on our eyes as cucumbers.

MOMMY: So you pretended you were at the spa?

CHLOE: Know what I'm saying?

MOMMY: Anything else?

CHLOE: And thank you for my family, and one more thing, huh, what is it? Oh, thank you for Mommy. Amen.

BARBIE DREAMS

Our ability to engage in fantasy is one of the first things we lose as we get older. In today's world, I think in great part due to the distractions of the Internet, video games, and television, kids seem to be losing their interest in fantasy earlier than ever. Chloe happens to be one of these kids who has retained her ability to suspend disbelief long after her friends and big sister have cast this interest aside.

"I'm a cat," she said to me matter-of-factly. The tissue paper tail tucked into the back of her pants that was trailing behind her was evidence of this transformation.

"I can see that," I said, looking up from the sink where I was washing dishes. "What is your name?"

"I don't know, but do you want to hear me meow?" she asked.

"Absolutely," I said, shutting off the water to give her my full attention.

"Meeeeeeeeeeow," she said in a high-pitched tone from somewhere in the back of her throat that strangely sounded exactly like a real cat.

Not only do I think her ability to engage in fantasy play is creative, but it's also very healthy. I think when children do nothing but sit in front of the television or the computer it makes them less creative, less curious, and in general, less interested in the world around them.

The spa game was one of my favorites. I'm not sure where she and her friend Taylor got the idea to put yogurt on their faces and grapes on their eyes, but I love the fact that they came up with something that mimics true life, and then made it a reality with the help of their imaginations.

I played with Barbies long after my friends had packed them away in boxes and sent them to the attic. I was painfully aware that playing with Barbies after a certain age was no longer cool, so I hid them in my closet and only brought them out when my cool friends were not around. For me, it was a chance to make up stories with real characters that mirrored real life. It was probably a strong foreshadowing of my becoming a writer.

"Mommy, will you play with me?" Chloe said to me one day recently with two Barbies in her hands. "You can be whichever one you want." I was torn between the blond in the ballerina dress with the close-cropped hair courtesy of Chloe's handiwork, or the dark beauty sporting a cute checkered retro bathing suit and matching cover-up.

"Of course I will," I said, putting down the laundry I was folding and dropping to my knees on the floor. Secretly, I was a little thrilled that it was finally cool to play with Barbies again. But it was also God's way of telling me as a parent that it is always cool to play with your child—that is something that never goes out of style.

CHLOE: Dear God and Jesus, thank you for going to the Hannah Montana concert. My favorite was "Boom Boom Clap." And Daddy's was "The Climb." What was yours, Mommy?

MOMMY: I think mine was "Party in the U.S.A."

CHLOE: And Mommy's was "Party was in the U.S.A." And I don't know what Mallory's is.

MOMMY: She said it was "The Climb."

CHLOE: Mallory's was actually "The Climb" too. Thank you for Thanksgiving and going to eat breakfast at Grammy's on Thanksgiving and getting to see a parade at Vi's.

MOMMY: What else did you do over the weekend? You saw a movie.

CHLOE: Getting to see a movie, *Christmas Carol*, with Cici, Livi.

MOMMY: You went to a party.

CHLOE: Going to Kelly's party. She gave me finger puppets of God and Jesus and Mary and the sheep and the lamb and the angel.

MOMMY: And you had a sleepover.

CHLOE: Having a sleepover with Cici.

MOMMY: And we went to church, that was fun.

CHLOE: How?

MOMMY: How was it fun? I don't know. You smiled a lot when we were there.

CHLOE: What did we do there again?

MOMMY: You went out in the line with the kids, and you had children's chapel. You like that.

CHLOE: Going to church and having to do a lot of stuff, and

thank you for my family, and one more thing, oh, thank you for Mommy. Amen.

THE FAMILY THAT ROCKS

It's amazing what parents endure for their children. As I write this, my kids are already over the Hannah Montana craze that captured their attention for at least a year. They have moved on to other teen Disney sensations. I really can't even begin to keep up with who is in and who is out.

"Selena Gomez is so pretty, Mommy," Chloe said to me. "And I think she probably looks like she's pretty nice too."

"I hope so, sweetie," I said, hoping silently that these teen idols won't disappoint their fans with bad behavior.

When we heard that Hannah Montana (a.k.a. Miley Cyrus) would be in Greensboro, North Carolina, about an hour and fifteen minutes away from where we live, we decided to get tickets and surprise the girls. Grif graciously agreed to go along. (He ended up being one of a handful of dads in a vast sea of mothers.) On the day of the show I went to the grocery store and picked up items for a tailgate picnic in the parking lot of the arena.

Best-laid plans—it poured. I don't mean just a little passing shower; I mean it was an absolute downpour. We actually stopped at a store on the way to the show to purchase umbrellas. Our festive picnic ended up happening inside the cramped car while the rain pounded down on the roof. We then dashed inside the arena, trying to keep from getting soaked as the rain seemed to be moving sideways in sheets.

Once inside, we prepared ourselves for what Grif and I both thought would be a painful evening watching a teen rock star bounce around the stage. At the very least, we were proving to our kids we could be *cool parents*. Secretly, I also wanted to know why this teen sensation had such a hold over young girls.

"Mommy, aren't you so excited?" Chloe asked me, tugging on my shirt as we sat in our seats anticipating the beginning of the concert.

"I sure am!" I said with a little too much faux enthusiasm.

As soon as the show started, the girls were on their feet mouthing the words to every song. Chloe had even dressed like Hannah Montana in a flouncy skirt with leggings and black boots and a shimmery top. Every time a song came on that she liked, she would grab my arm.

"Mommy, I *love* this song," she would squeal.

When it was all over, I had to admit that it was not as bad as I thought it was going to be. Seeing the concert through my daughters' eyes made the experience a lot more enjoyable than it otherwise would have been. I think in some ways that's yet another reason why God gives us children. Parenthood forces us to find new ways to look at the world around us, and sometimes we may even like what we see, or at the very least, learn to tolerate it.

Sometimes I catch myself as I drive home from work listening to Radio Disney. Admittedly, it was still tuned to the station from my morning commute with the girls to school. But it gives me comfort as I listen to the familiar tunes they belt out in the car every morning. Loving children means trying to be part of everything in their lives, the same way God inserts himself into our lives, seamlessly and without judgment.

CHLOE: Dear God and Jesus, thank you for going to the beach to stay in one of Vi's condos for four days and going to the swimming pool. And thank you for getting to work on my new place and getting to see Santa and go on the Polar Express, and the parade with the boats and seeing my friend Grace and stuff. Thank you for getting a little monkey toy, and thank you for my family, and one more thing, oh, thank you for Mommy, Daddy, and Sissy. Amen!

CLOSER TO HEAVEN

In the fall of 2008, my mother-in-law's husband died after a long illness. For years he had allowed us to use his old, ramshackle beach house on an island off the coast of North Carolina. In return, Grif and I and his sister and brother-in-law helped maintain the house and made small improvements along the way. But after his death, the house reverted to his daughter.

In the fall of 2009, we decided we would find a small, modest fixer-upper that could be our getaway—a place to go to escape all the chaos of our daily lives and just be together as a family. I envisioned having no television (I lost that battle) and no phone (I also lost that battle). After just one weekend of searching, we found the perfect family retreat.

"Mommy, it's like looking down from heaven," Chloe said of the view of the waterway and the marshland from our balcony.

"It sure is, baby," I said, thinking the same thing myself.

Our first weekend of work involved all of us ripping out the old carpet so that we could eventually put down hardwood floors. The girls helped us with what turned out to be a much bigger job than any of us expected. We rolled the old carpet and the padding up and placed it on a luggage cart for the six-floor journey down to the parking lot where we had a trailer waiting to take it to the local landfill. We repeated this cumbersome and tedious process over and over again for several hours until the floors were bare.

"Coming through," Chloe said as she pushed, dwarfed by the cart, and I pulled, trying to deftly maneuver it into the elevator.

What was so amazing about the experience was how hard the girls worked with no complaints. They clearly knew that we were embarking on a journey together, a journey that involved some hard work before we could reap the benefits of having a family retreat. At the time, I didn't really know how important the journey was going to be, how we would reconnect as a family in this place in a way that didn't seem possible when there was always laundry to fold, e-mails to answer, and closets to organize at home. There would be evenings spent playing games and watching movies together, days spent enjoying the open water as a school of dolphins showed us their tricks or a spectacular sunset convinced us that we really were a little closer to heaven. God was showing me that everything we needed was right here—in the heart of my family.

"You know why I like it here?" Chloe said to me one day.

"Why, baby?" I said as we cuddled under a blanket on a chaise lounge on the balcony just after sunset.

"Because it's small, not like our house at home. We're all together here," she said, nuzzling my neck.

I couldn't have said it any better.

CHLOE: Dear God and Jesus, thank you for getting to go to Vi's for four days, swimming in the swimming pool and stuff, and Mommy giving me yummy food to eat like Lucky Charms, and going to my other grandmother's to eat chicken, buns, and macaroni. And going back to school to see like Anna and Eden and stuff, those two people, and Nisma. And thank you for my family, and one more thing, oh, thank you for Mommy, Sissy, Daddy, Maddie, Pop Pop. Amen.

Giving Thanks

I usually work on Thanksgiving. I do this primarily because we all have to work one of the three big holidays in television, and I find this one to be the most benign. In past years, Grif has taken the girls to his stepmother's house to eat with his extended family, but in the fall of 2009 the plan changed.

I had originally agreed to work, but my boss told me that this year I would have the holiday off. I thought this was a pretty fortunate and rare opportunity for me to spend the day with my family. This particular year my husband had agreed to do two Thanksgivings—the traditional one with his stepmother midday in the town where he grew up, and a dinner at a restaurant that evening at the coast where his mother lived.

From the beginning, I sensed this was a bad idea. For one thing, my kids and I are not big eaters, so two meals so close together didn't appeal to me in any way. In addition, it sounded like a lot of rushing, not to mention travel time.

"But, Mommy, we just ate," Chloe said as we got in the car and informed her we were on our way to another Thanksgiving meal.

"I know, honey. But we're going to celebrate the holiday with your other grandmother now."

I started to regret that I had the holiday off. The Thanksgiving "lunch" had turned into a heavy late-afternoon feast. We then jumped in the car and rushed to the coast to a restaurant to meet his mother and sisters. The girls were exhausted and not a bit hungry. Chloe sat on my lap, her head on my shoulder, and eventually fell asleep in my arms. Mallory sat in the chair next to me and rested her head on my other shoulder. None of us but Grif ate, and he did so just to be polite. On the way to the hotel both girls suddenly woke up and naturally decided they were hungry.

"Mommy, I'm *starving*," Chloe wailed from the backseat. "I think I'm going to die."

"Probably not, sweetie, but we'll get you something to eat just in case," I said with a little more than a hint of sarcasm as my patience for the holiday was already threadbare.

It was Thanksgiving at the beach, so *nothing* was open, not even a drive-through. We ended up stopping at a convenience store and getting a box of Lucky Charms and some milk. I had long since banned Lucky Charms from my home, along with all other sugared cereal, in favor of healthier brands. But on this night getting Lucky Charms was about the luckiest thing that had happened to them all day. Given what little troopers they had been, I decided departing from our cereal routine for one weekend was not the end of the world.

"We love you, Mommy. Sooooo much. Thank you for getting us our favorite cereal," Chloe said, blowing me a kiss and then turning her attention back to her overflowing bowl of cereal.

In that moment I thought that while it wasn't exactly the Norman Rockwell Thanksgiving I had imagined, it was still a day spent with my family, an imperfect day that ended with a perfect moment of stillness only broken by the clinking of their spoons against the sides of their bowls. Suddenly, I forgot about wishing I was at work. I realized that God had given me this Thanksgiving as a gift, for me to understand what I truly had to be thankful for.

CHLOE: Dear God and Jesus, thank you for getting to read really, really, really good books and sitting by the fire when I read books, Christmas books. Having a sleepover with Cici like two days ago. What do you think?

MOMMY: How about going to the hockey game? That was good.

CHLOE: Going to the hockey game.

MOMMY: What did you do yesterday? You did something special. You went to a birthday party.

CHLOE: Someone's birthday party at Marbles, Marbles, Marbles. It's the awesomest place called Marbles. You know that. [Marbles is a children's museum in Raleigh, North Carolina.]

MOMMY: And thank you for almost being Christmas.

CHLOE: And thank you for it almost being Christmas. And thank you for my family, and one more thing, oh, thank you for Mommy.

THE REASON FOR THE SEASON

For children, the countdown to Christmas literally starts the second the decorations go up at the local mall. I used to get annoyed with the early Christmas mania—Christmas carols played incessantly on the radio, Christmas gear sharing an aisle with Halloween costumes at Target, and advertisements about pre-Christmas sales. But having children has changed my take on the countdown. I think the holiday season is something to enjoy and be cherished. Christmas is just one day, so why shouldn't everyone, especially kids, enjoy a prolonged walk-up to the big event?

"How many days?" Chloe asks me on a regular basis as we get into the month of December. Math is not my strong suit, so I usually have to consult the calendar along with a calculator.

Each year I have started getting out my Christmas decorations earlier and earlier. For one thing, I hate getting them out and then turning around a few short weeks later and putting them away. I decided that we should put the bulk of them out right after Thanksgiving and keep them up until after New Year's Day. Although, a few prized ones make it down from the attic even earlier in the month at Chloe's request. This allows all of us, including Chloe, who by now you know is a big fan of the "Jesus House," to really get into the holiday spirit.

"Is it time?" she asks me every year as I am putting the leftover turkey from her grandmother's house in the refrigerator.

"Almost," I say. "Ask Daddy."

"Daddy, Mommy says it's time!" she yells from the kitchen.

"Time for what?" he says, knowing full well what she is angling for.

"Time to put up Christmas!"

Chloe marvels at anything and everything that has to do with Christmas. Sure, she is excited about getting gifts, but she's equally excited about being an angel in the church Christmas pageant, about making Christmas cookies, and about seeing her extended family over the holidays. Probably what she is most excited about is *giving* gifts. Both she and Mallory begin making homemade gifts for the entire family weeks before Christmas. Suddenly, little crudely wrapped packages start appearing under the tree. Some of them contain homemade gifts; others are items that belong to them that they have decided to wrap and give away to each other.

"Chloe, you're really going to love this one," Mallory said, pointing to a small gift wrapped in newspaper on which she has drawn Chloe's name with purple magic marker.

"Oh, but, Mallory, *you're* going to love this one," Chloe said, holding up a package she had wrapped in tissue that appeared to have more tape than paper.

I have cast off my formerly "Bah Humbug" mantle and learned to enjoy the season as seen through my children's eyes. Every time I read a Christmas story to Chloe in front of the fireplace at night and she looks up at me full of light, I know what they mean when they talk about "the reason for the season."

CHLOE: Dear God and Jesus, thank you for going to ballet today and going to Alexa's and, and thank you for . . . Help . . .

MOMMY: Let's see. The rain making the flowers and the plants grow.

CHLOE: Making the rain because that means there might be snow.

MOMMY: And getting ready for your piano recital, that's exciting.

CHLOE: Getting ready for my piano recital and my Christmas pageant. And what else?

MOMMY: And seeing Sissy's concert this weekend.

CHLOE: And seeing Sissy's concert this weekend.

MOMMY: And how about your family?

CHLOE: Wait, what? Thank you for my family, and one more thing, oh, thank you for Mommy.

Show Stoppers

There are few times of the year that are busier than the Christmas season. There is the decorating, the shopping, the wrapping, the cards, and the planning of holiday celebrations. But now, as my children grow older I add one more thing to the list—*holiday shows*. As evidenced by Chloe's prayer, they have become just one more component of why she loves this time of year.

Mallory is in a city choir at a local college. They sing classical music and put on a holiday concert. In addition, both girls play piano and always have a winter recital just before Christmas. Finally, they have always participated in the Christmas pageant at church. It's hard to keep all of the rehearsals, outfits, and shows straight on my calendar, not to mention in my already crowded brain.

But to Chloe, the shows are an extension of how we celebrate Christmas. She beamed as Mallory and the Capital City Girls Choir took the stage in their little red jumpers and crisp white shirts. They are fresh faced with no makeup and their hair is pulled back. They look like they stepped straight out of *The Sound of Music* with their wholesome look that reminds me of a much simpler time.

"Mommy, there she is, there she is." Chloe pointed excitedly at her sister who is always in the back row because of her height. I started to shush her, and then realized everyone was turning around smiling to see who the sweet little sister was.

At the end of the show, Chloe couldn't wait to give her big sister a bouquet of flowers we had purchased at the grocery store on the way to the theater.

"Mommy picked them out," Chloe said to Mallory, not able to tell even the slightest fib. "But I carried them the whole time until now."

In the Christmas pageant at our new church, Mallory had finally gotten a coveted speaking part—Reader Three. She got to narrate the journey of a pregnant Mary with Joseph by her side into Bethlehem to the stable where she would give birth to the baby Jesus. Chloe was an angel in a crowded field of little girls clad in white sheaths with wings and silver tinsel halos. She had no interest in a speaking part, but she glowed as she floated down the aisle in her wings and halo because she saw us in the pew waving wildly at her and grinning from ear-to-ear. "Hi Mommy. Hi Daddy," she yell-whispered as she passed.

As I watched the stage crowded with little angels, shepherds, wise men, and more, my eyes suddenly shifted to the crowd of parents in the audience watching their children. It was in their eyes that I finally saw what pageant was truly all about—the transforming love parents have for their children, the same love God shares with us.

(*Chloe is in a bad mood.*)

CHLOE: (*unintelligible*)

MOMMY: Can't understand you. Losing a tooth?

CHLOE: Getting my second flu shot.

MOMMY: Getting your flu shot so you'll be safe and won't be sick. That's good. Getting your hair cut.

CHLOE: Getting my hair cut. Reading books. Amen.

MOMMY: Okay.

CHLOE: Not finished. Thank you for my family, and one more thing, oh, thank you for Sissy, Daddy, Mommy, Maddie, and Pop Pop. Amen.

DEVIL IN DISGUISE

Because she is so sweet most of the time, when Chloe is in a bad mood, or simply behaving badly, it's hard for me to handle. I just want my sweet girl back, and can't understand why she is acting the way she is. My frustration with her attitude only intensifies her annoyance with me, and she seems to slip even deeper into her negativity.

But what these moments really tell me is that Chloe, like the rest of us, is human. She is not a one-dimensional, perfect child, but a complex human being who is full of much more light than darkness, but has the capacity for brooding that exists in all of us. The truth is that I count on Chloe to lift me out of the doldrums with her positive outlook and seemingly boundless joy, so when she gets like this, it forces me to step up to the happyplate.

"Tell Mommy what's wrong," I say to her in these moments.

"You should know," she says cryptically. I start to go through all the possibilities—she's hungry, she's sad, or she has misplaced her favorite toy and thinks I threw it away.

Usually when she gets like this it is because she is tired. Young children clearly don't understand how weariness affects their moods. They only know that they don't feel well. As parents, we have to anticipate, understand, and learn how to handle these moments with as much diplomacy as possible. Most importantly, we have to learn how not to take it personally.

When a little devil comes out in Chloe, I know it won't last, that in the morning she will awake with her sunny disposition intact, the tension of the previous evening forgotten after a good night of sleep.

"You make Mommy so happy when I'm with you," I said to her the other day. "When are you happy?"

Chloe, who was holding my hand at the time, looked up at me quizzically, scrunched her nose, and rolled her little eyes.

"Mommy, I'm always happy," she said, squeezing my hand tightly. I returned the squeeze and smiled. *That's my girl*, I thought.

MOMMY: We have a lot to be thankful for. You want to say a nice prayer?

CHLOE: Dear God and Jesus, thank you for going to Grammy's and spending the night for one night and seeing my cousins and getting lots of toys. Like a box full of thank-you notes that you can write with, and Zhu Zhu Pets—which I always wanted my whole life. I got a Pet Shop House, my first one, and I put my Pet Shops in them. And there was one extra one in it.

MOMMY: Did you find some in your box? Some Pet Shops? (*Chloe's name for the little plastic Pet Shop animals she keeps in her Pet Shop House. She nods affirmatively to my question.*) Good.

CHLOE: They're all there. And thank you for this awesome baby doll. She has a bottle, baby wipes, and a pacifier and a bib, and a fork and spoon and my grandmother, Grammy, and Uncle Jim gave me the Pet Shop House, and the Pet Shops. Grammy gave me the Zhu Zhu Pets.

MOMMY: Grammy bought you the two best presents. Didn't she?

CHLOE: Can I make her cry once?

MOMMY: One time.

CHLOE: Watch. This is when she sucks her pacifier. (*crying noise*) See that?

MOMMY: That's pretty annoying.

CHLOE: I know. It really hurts your ears.

MOMMY: Makes you not want a baby until you are thirty, right?

CHLOE: But they wouldn't cry like that.

MOMMY: Your baby wouldn't cry like that, why? You cried

pretty hard when you were a baby. What else do you want
to thank God for? Who's coming to visit you tomorrow?

CHLOE: Thank you for my grandmother coming tomorrow,
Maddie. She's going to bring lots of presents. I'm so excited.
I'm so excited. Thank you for my family, one more thing,
oh, thank you for Mommy. Amen!

BABY DOLL DREAMS

Chloe couldn't stop playing with her baby doll during the prayer on this
night. It's a phenomenon I have a hard time relating to. I never liked
baby dolls as a child, and neither did Mallory. People would buy them
for her and she would immediately undress them, cut off their hair,
and draw on them with indelible black magic marker. Unfortunately,
Chloe, who *does* like baby dolls, inherited Mallory's less-than-savory
castoffs. She really wanted her very own new baby doll. When she
shared this with me one day leading up to Christmas, I told one of her
grandmothers that would be an ideal gift, and, boy, was I right.

"Mommy, all I want is a *real* baby doll. You know, the one who
cries and sucks on a pacifier," she said with pleading eyes.

"Really?" I asked, making sure I had heard her correctly.

"For real, Mommy," she replied.

From the moment Chloe opened the package with the baby doll
inside, it was in her arms. She carried it around with its accompanying
bag of baby items that included a change of clothes, wipes, a bottle,
and a pacifier. As I watched her nurture the fake baby, I realized that
Chloe's need to nurture is so deeply ingrained in her that even in fantasy play she gives it her all. She tenderly holds the baby doll on her
shoulder and burps her after a bottle. She takes a hat out of her bag
and puts it on the baby's head to keep it warm.

"Shush, Mama, the baby is sleeping. We don't want to wake her,"
she says in a hushed tone with complete sincerity as she motions to
the swaddled doll on her bed.

I often wondered if not playing with baby dolls would make me a bad mother, but somehow, even without that training, I figured out what to do. As a mother, I know it's important for me to honor Chloe's desire to play with dolls even if it wasn't my thing. As parents, we have to remember that even though our children come from our DNA, they are all unique individuals who have their own traits and interests that may be completely separate from our own. They are not little walking, talking mirror images of us—but one-of-a-kind human beings created by God in all his glory.

MOMMY: Chloe has a lot to be thankful for, so this might be a long one.

CHLOE: Dear God and Jesus, thank you for going to the pool. Wait. Where is the pool?

MOMMY: You went to the pool at the gym.

CHLOE: And going ice skating outside. And what else?

MOMMY: You saw the movie.

CHLOE: Thanks for seeing *Alvin and the Chipmunks*.

MOMMY: And you had lots of sleepovers. You had Cici. You had Aubie and Matthew.

CHLOE: Having a sleepover with my friend Cici, my cousin Aubie, and my friend Matthew.

MOMMY: I don't know. Did we thank God for all of the Christmas presents?

CHLOE: Thank you for the bouncy ball, my bike, my scooter, and everything else I don't remember, my grandmother, and my baby doll. And thank you for my family and one more thing, oh, thank you for Mommy, Daddy, Sissy, Pop Pop, Nonni, Vi, Daddy's daddy, whatever his name is.

MOMMY: It's Reginald.

CHLOE: Reginald. And thank you for God and Jesus. Amen.

CHLOE'S ANGELS

For as long as I can remember, Chloe has been fascinated with the concept of heaven. She asks me questions all the time about it. It's something that I have not been totally comfortable talking about because my own ideas about heaven are constantly evolving. But children want answers, and they depend on us to give them those answers.

"Will we be able to play in heaven?" she said one day from the backseat of the car as we were driving to ballet.

"I'm sure we will, honey," I replied, hoping the questions wouldn't get too much harder.

"Is it like a bunch of clouds that we jump around on?" she probed.

"I'm not sure, sweetie. Mommy has never been there," I responded, trying to be honest without crushing her curiosity.

But what she wants to know most often is, will she see the people she loves in heaven?

"I sure hope so," I told her, imagining how much my grandmother, Lady, would be delighted to meet both of my precious daughters.

The person she is perhaps the most curious about is the grandfather she never met—Grif's dad. Reggie died in 1993 of lung cancer, a year before I met Grif, so all of my stories to Chloe about her grandfather are based on Grif's description of his father. Chloe has asked about him on many occasions, and it makes her sad that she never got a chance to meet him. But in her heart, she believes she will meet him in heaven. On this night, when she brought him up in her prayer, it touched me. I knew that meant she was beginning to think of him as a real person.

"Mommy, Mallory has a question about heaven too," Chloe said with a grin that I spied after peeking in my rearview mirror at her.

"What is it, sweetie?" I asked.

"Is there a Target in heaven?"

"I sure hope so," I said. But what I really hoped for was that Chloe's version of heaven would be a real place, a place that was within all of our reach.

4

NESTING

The color of springtime is in the flowers, the color of winter is in the imagination.

—TERRI GUILLEMETS

MOMMY: Chloe's getting ready to go back to school tomorrow. She's telling me her favorite animals for her prayer tonight. She wants to thank God for all the animals. Chloe, what are your favorite animals in order?

CHLOE: Mine is—I just made this up—bunny, monkey, what goes next?

MOMMY: I don't know, you had frog and rhinoceros.

CHLOE: Frog and hippo actually.

MOMMY: Those are pretty good animals.

CHLOE: In order like, two, three, four.

MOMMY: What do you want to thank God for?

CHLOE: Thank you for the winter break and thank you for Christmas, the awesomest time of the year.

MOMMY: Are you thankful to go back and see your friends tomorrow?

CHLOE: Thank you for going to school tomorrow. Kind of happy, and kind of sad.

MOMMY: What are you sad about?

CHLOE: I have to get up so early.

MOMMY: What's the happy part?

CHLOE: I get to see my friends. And thank you for all the presents people gave me, and Allison giving me those fun, fun books, and my puppies in my pocket, awesome, awesome. Where are my puppies, in my pockets? [She is referring to small plastic toy puppies she got in her Christmas stocking.]

MOMMY: I don't know. I haven't touched them. Anything else you want to thank God for? Your family?

CHLOE: Thank you for Mommy, Daddy, Pop Pop, Vi, Nonni, Daddy's daddy, Maddie, Otto, Grammy.

MOMMY: That's a lot of people.

CHLOE: I've already did Vi, Nonni, and everybody else in the whole world. I still like bad guys. I don't like how they act.

MOMMY: That's good. You love them even when they're bad.

CHLOE: No, I don't like them, how they're mean, but I still like them.

MOMMY: That's pretty nice.

CHLOE: Amen.

LOVING THE BAD GUYS

One thing adults are pretty bad at is loving people we don't really like. Jesus said to "love your neighbor as yourself," but it is one of the hardest commandments to follow. In recent years, this has become especially difficult for me to do with the proliferation of constant criticism of journalists online by anonymous posters.

Chloe had obviously heard me talking about the "bad guys" that Mommy does stories on as a crime reporter for the television news. Without my even knowing it, she had formed an opinion that, despite their actions, they still deserved her love. This was not something that I taught her. I taught her to stay away from "bad guys," to look out for "bad guys," and to feel sorry for "bad guys" when their life circumstances led them down the wrong path. But making the leap to loving "bad guys" was definitely God's doing, not mine.

"Mommy, they can't always help themselves," she said to me one day when I was giving her a stern lecture about not wandering away from me in public. "I know we have to stay away from them, but we don't have to be mean to them."

I think oftentimes when we point out bad qualities in others, we are actually looking in a mirror and recognizing negative traits in ourselves. In order to love other people, we have to love ourselves first. In some ways, this is probably even harder to do than loving our neighbors.

"I love myself, Mama," Chloe has said to me on more than one occasion. And I know she means it, not in an arrogant way, but in the way God intended us to feel about ourselves as we are reflections of his love.

Chloe is teaching me to love myself more, and my neighbors, and even the "bad guys." I'm still working on loving the people who post mean comments on my blog—*maybe someday.*

CHLOE: Dear God and Jesus, thank you for going back to school today, having ballet, and seeing my babysitter for the first time in a long time, and Allison gave me three new books for Christmas, and I read a whole book by myself until when I was almost finished when Mallory barged in and had to sing so loud. And I never read a book to Mommy that's really big when Mallory didn't barge in. Next time can we lock the door?

MOMMY: Start thinking about thanking God for things.

CHLOE: Thank you for my family and one more thing, oh, thank you for everybody in the world.

MOMMY: Especially?

CHLOE: Oh, thank you for Mommy. Amen.

SHARING THE SPOTLIGHT

If there's one thing Mallory knows how to do well, it's steal the spotlight. She barged into Chloe's room during prayers because she didn't like the attention I was giving her little sister, attention she felt was being taken away from her. It wasn't the first time she had tried to disrupt our prayer time.

From a very young age, Mallory wasn't very interested in praying out loud together at night. When she did, it was usually a scripted prayer. She tells me now that she prefers to say prayers to herself in her head at night. I have respected this preference, hoping that she will come at her own faith in a way that is comfortable for her. She also started reading to herself when she was little and really didn't want me to read to her or put her to bed. Most of the time, I am telling her to turn out her light as she begs me to let her read one more chapter.

"Sweetie, it is very late. You're always so tired in the morning," I say.

"But it's getting really good; let me just finish this chapter," she pleads.

Most of my time spent with Mallory at night involves helping with homework and school projects. Even though I consider these to be loving moments between a parent and a child, for Mallory, it is not the same as my sharing the bedtime ritual with Chloe, a ritual in which she does not want to engage, but also doesn't want Chloe to engage in either if it means getting my attention. I'm still working on balancing their separate needs for my attention. I'm getting better at negotiating the boundaries, but it is still a work in progress.

"You always spend, like, ten minutes with me, and, like, forty with her," Mallory has said defensively on more than one occasion.

"Not true, young lady. We just spent an hour on your school project. Why doesn't that count?" I respond, knowing I will never win this debate. I want to remind her of all the nights we spent doing the bedtime ritual together before Chloe came along, and even afterward when Chloe was an infant and sleeping soundly as I read to Mallory, said prayers with her, and cuddled. Sometimes I want to make her sit down and watch twenty straight hours of home videos of her babyhood into toddlerhood into childhood so she can truly see that I love her just as much as her sister and shared the same tender moments with her that I now share with Chloe.

In Chloe's mind, she has always played second fiddle to Mallory's big personality. She simply wants a few minutes of my undivided attention every night. Even at a very young age, she was telling me that she needed "one-on-one" time with me and that there were things she needed to speak to me "privately" about. I cherish the fact that Chloe wants to spend time with me and trusts me enough to share private things, but I also have another child whom I need to love as fiercely and give my attention to just as passionately.

In my heart I believe God gives us the strength as mothers to be the best parents we can be to all our children and to figure out how to create the best possible balance of love for our family's needs. If I'm wrong, I might just have to clone myself.

CHLOE: Dear God and Jesus, thank you for Mallory's birthday, I think in about three days, right? And thank you for presents for Christmas and going back to school and having a sleepover with Aubie. For Mallory's birthday I'm going to do everything. Me and Aubie are having a sleepover on her birthday, except for all the girls are sleeping downstairs, and me and Aubie are sleeping upstairs. Thank you for my family, and one more thing, oh, thank you for Mommy, Daddy, and Sissy. Amen.

Birthday Blues

The hardest time to be a little sister is when you are being told you can't do something because you are not old enough. On Mallory's ninth birthday she had a slumber party, and we shipped Chloe off to her cousin Auburn's house for the night so that she would not interrupt the festivities. I heard about this for the next year from Chloe as one of the biggest missed opportunities in her life. So, on Mallory's tenth birthday, we decided to compromise. We told Chloe that she could be part of the next party, but when it was time to turn out the lights and go to sleep in the party room, she and her cousin would have to retire to her bedroom upstairs.

"I promise we'll be good, Mommy. We won't embarrass Mallory. We'll act like big girls," she told me in the days leading up to the party.

Mallory was not thrilled with this arrangement, especially because her friends tend to think Chloe is so cute that they sometimes play with her and ignore Mallory. And, of course, there was Mallory's perception that it was *her* party and Chloe was crashing it. We pointed out that Mallory had never been excluded from any of Chloe's birthday parties.

"Well, then she's not coming to *my* birthday party," Chloe said defiantly when Mallory lobbied to keep her out, her little hands perched squarely on her hips. But after some tense negotiations, they both caved in and agreed to my compromise. As it turned out, Chloe and her cousin fit right in with the big girls that night. They played dress-up with them, danced with them, and even stayed awake for the movie and popcorn. Mallory actually seemed proud to show off her little sister's undying admiration for her. After the movie was over, I ushered Chloe and her cousin upstairs to her room. She didn't seem concerned that she would be missing anything in the basement. In fact, she told me that she knew her bed would be more comfortable than sleeping on the cold, hard floor in a sleeping bag.

As I've said before, these moments convince me that God does have a plan for these two sisters, a plan that involves a lifetime of friendship and a bond of unconditional love. Slowly, we were feeling our way there together, one prayer at a time.

CHLOE: Dear God and Jesus, thank you for, thank you for, thank you for Mallory's party yesterday, having cake, a cupcake, and my cousins and friends, and Mommy baking the cake and Beth bringing the cupcakes, and . . . Help . . .

MOMMY: Playing outside in your little Fairytale Land.

CHLOE: Playing outside in Terabithia.

MOMMY: What is your name?

CHLOE: I am Princess Nature.

MOMMY: And what is your sister?

CHLOE: Princess Sunlight.

MOMMY: And you and I have a new club, don't we?

CHLOE: Yeah. We're trying to teach Mallory to be polite.

MOMMY: Do you think it's going to work?

CHLOE: But we're going to have to work on it a lot. I'm going to write down in my notebook. And we're going to write down what she does, and then we're going to make the things that she does bad better, and then we check it when she does it better.

MOMMY: That's a good idea. Do you think it's going to work? Possibly?

CHLOE: Maybe. Maybe.

MOMMY: Anything else you want to thank God and Jesus for?

CHLOE: Thank you for reading books with Daddy. Going in the backyard and playing in the woods. Thank you for my family, and oh, one more thing, thank you for Mommy. Amen!

Team Politeness

Mallory has always had a toughness about her that protects her from getting her feelings hurt, but also sometimes projects an image to the world that she is indifferent to others' feelings. While I don't believe this to be true in her heart, she doesn't always come across as compassionate, something Chloe worries a lot about when it comes to her big sister. To this end, Chloe decided she would take on the task of helping soften Mallory's rough edges.

"Mommy, she really does have a good heart. She can be really nice to me. We just have to get her to show it more," Chloe said as she tried to convince me her plan was a good one.

Unlike a parent whose brilliant ideas are usually categorically shut down by children, siblings can sometimes reach each other in ways that we cannot. Chloe told me that she would model more compassionate behavior to her sister and show her that you get more with sugar than vinegar.

I admit, I was skeptical about Chloe's approach, but at the same time I thought, how could it hurt?

"You know how she is," Chloe would often say when Mallory did something that hurt her feelings. "That's just Mallory."

But amazingly, in the past year Mallory has blossomed into a young lady who will look you in the eye, smile, and shake your hand. She will even exchange pleasantries over the phone or in person with an adult when the situation calls for it. I am so impressed with how she has adapted her tough-as-nails exterior into something a little bit softer and gentler. Don't get me wrong, she is still a pistol, but now she knows how to be in the world with others in a way that makes me proud. And I'm not the only one who sees it.

"Mallory has been really good lately," Chloe says on a regular basis now with pride.

I know that the majority of this transformation is simple maturity, but I can't help but think that we take so many of our social cues from the people around us, the people closest to us. I think in the end, Chloe makes Mallory a little bit kinder and more sensitive to others' needs. By the same token, Mallory makes Chloe more thick-skinned and adventurous than she would otherwise be. God put them together for a reason—they bring out the best in one another.

And they definitely bring out the best in me.

CHLOE: Dear God and Jesus, thank you for going bowling, the balloon show yesterday, and going upstairs [at the gym] to exercise with Mommy, to exercise with Mommy, Daddy, and Brooke and Connor and their mom. There's like bouncy things. I felt like I was going to die.

MOMMY: Because you were tired. You did so well, though. I was so proud of you. You did so well. Your face was a little red.

CHLOE: I know. It was a lot red.

MOMMY: What else? We went to the beach. You got to swim in the indoor pool.

CHLOE: Going to the beach, and thank you for my family, and one more thing, oh, thank you for Mommy, Daddy, and Sissy. Amen.

MOMMY: Should we ask God to help the people in Haiti because of the earthquake?

CHLOE: Help Haiti get better. I want them to be like us. Not too rich, but we have lots.

MOMMY: We're just right, huh?

CHLOE: Yes. Amen.

ALL GOD'S CHILDREN

Chloe has always embraced the phrase "all God's children." She truly has no boundaries when it comes to thinking about people who may be dealing with tragedy anywhere in the world. Because we tend to watch news in our house, and she goes to a very socially conscious school where they talk about the global needs of others, she has always been very tuned in to what is going on in the world.

"We're raising money for the people in Haiti at school," she told me.

"That's great," I said, not looking up from my computer.

"Can you help me?" she said with a strained voice. I looked over to see her struggling to get the bottom off of her piggy bank.

When Hurricane Katrina hit, Chloe was just two and a half years old. I made three separate trips to the area in the year following the storm covering the aftermath of the disaster. It was around this time that she was learning to say bedtime prayers out loud, and she incorporated praying for the hurricane victims into her prayer every night. Even a year after the tragedy, when many people had already forgotten about the Gulf states, Chloe was still praying for them every night.

"Don't forget the hurricane victims," she would say as I tried to rush her to the "amen."

The earthquake in Haiti became even more real to her because she was older and truly understood some of the images she was seeing on television. What I especially loved about her take on the situation on this night was that she wanted them to have enough money to be comfortable, "like us," but not "rich." In Chloe's heart she truly believes we have everything we need, and that's the simple dream she had for the people of Haiti.

Once again, I was learning from her basic six-year-old wisdom. God doesn't want us to use money as our standard for happiness and success because most of us already have what we need right in front of us. I know I do.

CHLOE: Dear God and Jesus, thank you for getting a new baby doll for my prize for earning my chips today because I didn't get a prize and Mallory did. Mallory got cranky because she didn't get something today, but she already got it, right? And thank you for painting my rocks. I'm finishing them all today, painting a hundred rocks. What's next?

MOMMY: Reading some really good books.

CHLOE: Reading really, really, really good books.

MOMMY: Like *The Wizard of Oz*.

CHLOE: Like reading two pieces of *The Wizard of Oz*, and thank you for my family, and one more thing, oh, thank you for Mommy. Amen.

KNOW WHEN TO HOLD 'EM

As parents we employ lots of different tricks to get our children to behave and act like civilized human beings. Believe me, I've done it all—chore charts, allowance, bribery, you name it. On one occasion a friend mentioned to me that she had a system where she put a red jelly bean in a jar when her children did their assigned chores every day. If they didn't do what they were asked to do, or stepped out of line by doing something like talking back, she put a black jelly bean in the jar. They then had to work off the black jelly beans in order to get back in good graces. Seven red jelly beans meant a prize worth less than five dollars. They could also save up their earnings and get a larger prize if that's what they chose to do.

"I can do that, Mommy," Chloe said after I explained the concept to her. "I probably won't get any bad ones."

"Let's hope not," I said, rubbing the top of her head.

I created my own system with poker chips. Same concept, different delivery method. The problem was that the girls usually didn't have their seven chips at the same time, so they didn't get prizes at the same time. Chloe also liked to save up her chips and get an even bigger prize. Mallory—Miss Immediate Gratification—wanted to run to the store instantly upon winning the coveted seventh chip and spend her money before it burned a hole in her pocket.

When Chloe saved up and got a baby doll, Mallory was not a happy camper. Chloe gloated a little, proudly carrying the doll around the house for several days. Mallory stewed, refusing to make eye contact with Chloe while she was holding the doll, a doll that Mallory would never have wanted in a million years, but it still steamed her that her sister had saved up for a bigger prize.

God gave me two very different children for a specific reason. He wants us as parents to learn different things from each of our children, and learn how to parent unique children with completely opposite personalities. It's a daily challenge. I think I am finally coming to terms with their individual needs—loving them equally, but differently.

Like so many other good ideas, the poker chip reward system has gone by the wayside. I now tell my children they need to do their chores and listen to what I say because that's part of the responsibility of being in a family. "Is it working?" you ask. The jury is still out.

CHLOE: Dear God and Jesus, thank you for getting to go to Macaroni Grill. I paid with my own money by doing jobs. And guess what? Guess what?

MOMMY: What?

CHLOE: I made my own pizza. And we got to draw on the table.

MOMMY: Did everybody have as many jobs as you or no?

CHLOE: Mommy, my teacher was impressed. People, they had jobs and mostly got twenty-five cents, thirty cents, like sixty cents and one dollar. That's all they had to do. I filled up the list.

MOMMY: So she thought that was good?

CHLOE: They were impressed.

MOMMY: You're a hard worker.

(*She starts giggling uncontrollably.*)

MOMMY: Come on, sweetie. Let's get serious.

CHLOE: I love crabby paddies. Thank you for watching a little *American Idol*, and thank you for my family, and one more thing, oh, thank you for Mommy, Daddy, Sissy, Vi, Maddie, Nonni, Grammy, Pop Pop, Daddy's daddy.

MOMMY: How come you used to just say Mommy, and now you say all these people?

CHLOE: Because Mallory always comes in.

MOMMY: But she's not here now.

CHLOE: Yeah, but she's probably listening.

MOMMY: So you don't want her to feel bad by leaving her out? That's nice. Should we pray for all the people in Haiti?

CHLOE: One more thing, I hope the Haiti people will get all the money the schools are raising. I hope they can get better soon. So they can at least buy a hospital and other needs if they have a little money left. Everybody. Amen. Remember Haiti. Nighty night.

SHE WORKS HARD FOR THE MONEY

For a class project, the first grade teachers asked us to assign our children small chores around the house and pay them. The goal was for each child to earn six dollars, and then have them take that on a field trip to a local restaurant where they would use it to pay for their lunch.

The instructions were to have children do many small tasks for small sums of money. Chloe, naturally, took this to heart.

"What do you think folding a whole basket of laundry is worth, Mama?" Chloe asked me.

"I don't know," I said, struggling to come up with a fair number. In my head I was thinking, *I'm so tired, I'd give anything for someone to fold this for me.* "Fifty cents?"

"Nope, too high. How about twenty-five cents?" she replied, putting her hand to her head like she was thinking.

At first I thought she was devaluing herself, and then I realized she was just following the letter of the assignment to a T. She didn't want it to be easy. She wanted to *work* for the money.

It's funny when you have a child who looks nothing like you; you wonder where the shared DNA is hidden. I mean, I saw her come out of my womb. She's my baby. But she looks *exactly* like her daddy. There's not a shred of me in her appearance. But I see glimpses of me in her personality. I definitely inherited the Puritan work ethic gene from my parents, and it looks like Chloe has gotten it from me.

"Anything else you need me to do?" she would ask in the days leading up to the field trip. "I can Windex something."

I was so proud of Chloe for working so hard for her pizza money. Even more importantly, I was proud that she was proud, that she knew she had really accomplished something. Parenting in a chaotic world is all about the small victories, and with God's help we are able to recognize them for the blessings they are.

CHLOE: Dear God and Jesus, hope Haiti gets better with all the money the school is donating. Everybody, these kids gave, like, three hundred dollars.

MOMMY: What would you buy in Haiti if you had some money? What would you help them with?

CHLOE: I would buy food, and I would buy a house and put new stuff in it. And clothing.

MOMMY: That's good.

CHLOE: Thank you for all the sledding and the school delay.

MOMMY: Are you glad for your delay? And you didn't get to have school yesterday.

CHLOE: Thank you for getting to go to ballet today and going to get my costume for the recital. It's in May.

MOMMY: Snow White costume.

CHLOE: Remember last year it was on Daddy's birthday. Wasn't it on his birthday?

MOMMY: Uh-huh.

CHLOE: I thought it was on his birthday this year.

MOMMY: It's not, it's on May 22.

CHLOE: Who is the closest birthday to that?

MOMMY: Daddy's birthday is close to that, but it's not on it. You want to thank God for your family?

CHLOE: Thank you for my family, and one more thing, thank you for Mommy coming back because she left really early and came back pretty much really late when I was asleep. Like at midnight probably. That reminds me. I need to check the clock more. Thank you for my family and one more thing, thank you for Mommy, Daddy, Vi, Nonni, Maddie, Pop Pop, Daddy's daddy, Aunt Nancy, Vi, Alexa, Amy,

Auburn, Uncle Paul, Purple Buddy, Blue Buddy. Didn't we
once have, like, Orange or Red Buddy?

MOMMY: Just say amen. You're driving me crazy, girl. Say amen.

CHLOE: (*singing*) Amen.

Prayer Train

Somehow, over the course of the year, the prayers had become part
of an extended conversation between Chloe and me with a lot of very
specific details about her day thrown in. It was becoming increasingly harder to keep her on track because she wanted to fit every
little tidbit of her life into the prayer so that she could share everything with me. Truth be told, I loved hearing about her day; I just
wanted to make sure we were still focusing on the mission, which was
to thank God for our many blessings.

"Why don't we talk a little first so you can get everything out
before we pray?" I would sometimes say.

"Mommy, I want to save it all for the prayer," she said as if
talking first might amount to rehearsing what was meant to be
ad-libbed.

Haiti was dominating the news, so it was no surprise to me that it
was still dominating Chloe's heart and mind. While I know my job is
to try and keep her prayer train on the tracks, at the same time, I realize that every little twist and turn in her day most often reflects her
thankfulness to God.

The prior year she was sad that her father's birthday fell on the
same day as her dance recital—not for herself, but for him. She hated
the fact that his birthday was overshadowed by her dance recital, and
wanted to make sure we still celebrated his birthday. In this year, she
was very thankful to God that her dance recital would not conflict
with her father's birthday.

She was also thankful for me coming home, albeit late. Chloe
always tries to stay up and wait for me when I am working late. On

these rare occasions, I always call her and ask her about her day and then tell her that she needs to go to bed before I get home.

"But, Mommy, I miss you. When are you coming home?" she asks.

I always come in and kiss both of them no matter what time it is, pull their covers up, and whisper in their ears, "Mommy loves you." Sometimes, one or both of them will crack a faint smile even though I know they are still fast asleep.

Creating the balance between the mission and the method is something I am getting better at one prayer at a time. I hope my children will always want to share with me the details of their day far beyond the time when they leave the nest and go off into the world.

CHLOE: Dear God and Jesus, thank you for letting Mallory getting her ears pierced. Having a really good school day today.

MOMMY: Daddy getting to Nevada safely?

CHLOE: And thank you for Daddy going to somewhere really safely. I miss him.

MOMMY: You miss Daddy?

CHLOE: I hope he comes back.

MOMMY: He'll come back, baby.

CHLOE: What if he dies?

MOMMY: Don't say that. Nothing is going to happen to Daddy. We love Daddy.

CHLOE: Or gets hurt, gets injured.

MOMMY: He won't, baby. He'll be safe.

CHLOE: Mommy, I don't know what to say.

MOMMY: How about just thanking God for your family?

CHLOE: Thank you for my family, and one more thing, oh, thank you for Mommy, Daddy, and Sissy and everybody else. Amen.

The Missing Piece

I've said it before, and it's really true: the one thing I can't be to my girls is a father, and likewise, he can't be a mother. Grif doesn't travel much for work, so when he is away, I try to make it a fun time for the girls to take their minds off his absence. We usually pile into our king-size bed, watch a movie, and sleep together, albeit with a lot of shifting on my part as little legs and arms invade my space like octopus tentacles and push me to the edge of the bed.

But Chloe has a difficult time when her daddy is not around. At first, she enjoys the special perks of his absence—the treats, staying up late, sleeping with Mommy—but that fades when he is gone for more than a day or two. To most children, there is nothing like the comfort of a family to make them feel safe in the world. A family is like a puzzle; when one piece is missing, it does not feel complete.

"When is Daddy coming home?" she asks every day.

"Soon, sweetie," I tell her, gently stroking her back.

"But I really miss him," she says with tears forming at the corners of her eyes.

On this particular night, Grif had traveled out west to go skiing with a group of friends with whom he had grown up. He had taken a trip like this every few years since we had been married, but Chloe was so young the last time, she didn't remember it. Therefore, this trip wasn't sitting well with her. She wasn't used to her father being gone for an entire week.

Chloe's paranoia about something bad happening to her father was very real. I wanted to reassure her that he would be okay. But the reality is that we never know for sure what will happen from one day to the next, especially considering Grif's lack of skiing ability combined with his delusions of grandeur in this area that often led him to ski runs that were way above his skill level.

Being in the news business has taught me to be prepared for anything. One minute someone is just living his or her life; the next minute a plane crashes or an earthquake happens, and everything changes in an instant. So, at the end of the day, all we can really do is ask God for his help in keeping our loved ones safe as they leave home and venture out into the world.

Grif did, of course, come home to his family safely and complete the puzzle, and I have no doubt that Chloe's prayers to this end every single night helped make that happen. He had a little angel riding on his shoulder as he zoomed down those black diamond runs.

Chloe on Daddy:

If I need help fixing something he would do it. He's like a big pillow, like a bear. I love him because he's funny. He always makes me laugh. He makes me feel safe.

CHLOE: Dear God and Jesus, thank you for getting these cool books from book order. One of them has stickers. And thank you for . . .

MOMMY: Have you had any special visitors in your house this week? Guests?

CHLOE: Oh, and Maddie coming, and she brought the cupcakes, the delicious cupcakes, and she puts chocolate on our bed every night.

MOMMY: What did you do this afternoon after school? You went somewhere.

CHLOE: And thank you for going to ballet today.

MOMMY: What else? Your family?

CHLOE: And thank you for my family. And one more thing, oh, thank you for Daddy, Mommy, Maddie, and Mallory. Amen.

MADDIE: That was wonderful!

I Heart Chocolate

I always tell my children that you love someone because of how they make you feel, not because of what they give you. But this is a hard concept for children to grasp when it comes to grandparents. Part of the fun of being a grandparent is indulging your grandchildren, and as Chloe mentioned in this prayer, my mother puts chocolate on their pillows every night when she is visiting to make them feel like they are staying in a fancy hotel.

"Mommy, look!" Chloe says with unbridled enthusiasm as she picks up the little chocolate wrapped delicately in gold paper. She always acts as if it is a big surprise to her, when in reality she anticipates it from the moment my mother walks in the door.

In my heart, I know the girls' love for Maddie is a whole lot deeper than cupcakes and chocolate, but it is hard for them to express this while they are seduced by the lure of her goodies. And so while Chloe thanks God for the things Maddie brings her, I silently thank God for *my* mother.

"And one more thing, oh, *thank you for Mom.*"

CHLOE: Dear God and Jesus, thank you for Lent starting today, and I'm giving up apple juice and orange juice, which is a big deal. It's hard to not drink orange juice and apple juice. Thank you for getting to have a playdate with Cici and going to her birthday party in three days. It is February the . . .

MOMMY: The twentieth.

CHLOE: February twentieth.

MOMMY: And who else is coming to visit you?

CHLOE: And thank you for Pop Pop coming to visit me tomorrow.

MOMMY: Day after tomorrow.

CHLOE: Day after tomorrow.

MOMMY: I'm coming to your class tomorrow morning.

CHLOE: And Mommy reading books with me.

MOMMY: Thank you for my family, and one more thing, oh, thank you for Mommy, Daddy, and Sissy and everybody else that's good. Amen.

FORTY DAYS IN THE DESERT WITHOUT CHOCOLATE

You would think the concept of Lent would be a hard one for children to grasp. But Chloe seemed to understand right away that it had to do with Jesus' sacrifice for us and his fasting for forty days in the desert in preparation for Holy Week. Lent starts on Ash Wednesday and ends on Easter. While historically giving up something was a tradition unique to Catholics and Episcopalians, it has now caught on in other Protestant denominations.

Chloe thought long and hard about what she would give up this year after I explained to her that it should be something she would really miss. At the same time, I didn't want to pressure her. I wanted it to be her decision.

"Mommy, it would be very hard for me to give up juice, because you know how much I like it," she told me as she was working through her choice out loud.

"I know, honey. But that's the whole point of Lent, to give up something you will really miss," I said gently, trying to nudge, but not push her into making a decision.

While I have always given up something for Lent—a tradition instilled in me at a young age by my parents and the church I attended as a child—I didn't broach the subject with my girls until they were old enough to actually understand the concept.

Usually I give up desserts, which for someone with a sweet tooth is no easy task. I especially miss chocolate, which I consider to be its own separate food group. I often refer to this time of year as "Forty Days in the Desert Without Chocolate."

"I guess I could just drink milk and water. I like milk, and it's good for me, so that would be okay? Right, Mommy?" Chloe said, again trying to work it out in her own mind.

This was the first year that Chloe truly bought into the whole idea. Of course, we had to make some exceptions. I told her that if she was at someone's house and they only offered her juice, then she had no choice but to drink it. Chloe decided to give up orange juice because she thought she had in essence become a juice-a-holic and needed to dial it back.

"Mommy, it is so hard. I really want some orange juice, but I don't want to disappoint God," she said on a daily basis throughout Lent.

Rather than focusing on the guilt, I wanted her to focus on the sacrifice. In my own head I would hear, *God is proud of you for giving up that yummy-looking, gooey chocolate chip cookie.* I am saying this of course over and over again as my taste buds salivate and my stomach lurches with a hunger pain that only chocolate has the power to cure.

"Sweetie, God knows it's hard. And he's proud of you. Just think, on Easter you can have all the orange juice you want!" I said cheerfully. And I was proud of her too. Discipline is one of the toughest mountains to scale in life. Thankfully, it is something that has always come to me naturally, especially as it relates to things like meeting work deadlines and exercising. As a rule, discipline is a learned behavior for Chloe, but I'm realizing as discipline applies to faith, she is leading, and I am following.

MOMMY: Here's Chloe Bear.

CHLOE: Dear God and Jesus, thank you for, let's see, Pop Pop coming tomorrow.

MOMMY: And the beautiful sunshine today.

CHLOE: No, it was windy.

MOMMY: And getting a new book.

CHLOE: And getting a new book. Oh, and Mommy coming to talk about her job at school. How long is Pop Pop staying?

MOMMY: Three whole days.

CHLOE: Just three? Maddie stayed for, like, a week.

MOMMY: Yep. But Pop Pop is staying for three, so you should be thankful for that.

CHLOE: Why can't he stay more?

MOMMY: Because that's as long as he can stay. He's got to go back to work. How about your family?

CHLOE: Thank you for my family, and one more thing, oh, thank you for my family, my whole entire family. Amen.

And the River Don't Rise

When you live roughly four hundred and fifty miles away from your parents, and they still work full-time, it is hard to arrange time to get together. We do an annual two-week vacation to the Jersey Shore where we spend one week with my father (Pop Pop) and his wife (Nonni), and one week with my mother (Maddie). My father also makes one annual trip to visit us in February to see an ACC basketball game.

My father was a typical 1970s-era dad. I saw him at the dinner table and occasionally at one of my school events. Like most fathers in that time period, he was not around much because he worked a lot. At the time, his absence was not unusual because hands-on parenting by fathers had not yet been invented. So it's no wonder that he wasn't exactly sure what to do with his granddaughters, especially when they were babies.

As they got older, my father became better at interacting with my girls because they were real people who could actually hold a conversation with him. But they still don't see him on a regular basis, so there is always a warming-up period when he arrives. Also, I still occasionally have to remind him to put down the iPad and pay attention to what the girls are saying. Chloe knows how to relate to Pop Pop in her own special way that melts him from an iPad-absorbed lawyer into a story-reading grandfather. Chloe is slowly realizing that even his short visits are special, something to cherish.

As I observe my parents as grandparents, I realize that if we're lucky, we really do get a second chance in life to love and nurture children. The beauty is that the second time around, as a grandparent, you have more wisdom and less anxiety. Being a grandparent is God's way of completing the circle of love in a family. Even though it is a long way away, I look forward to that stage in my life. As they say, "God willing, and the river don't rise," I will be around long enough to enjoy it.

CHLOE: Dear God and Jesus, thank you for . . .

MOMMY: Who came to visit you?

CHLOE: Pop Pop coming to our house to visit for a couple days. And thank you for what?

MOMMY: Cici's party.

CHLOE: Cici's party, having a sleepover with her even though they were throwing up. They all got sick from this milk except Owen, their baby brother.

MOMMY: And thank God for you not getting sick.

CHLOE: And thank you for me not getting sick. And Eddie, Livi, and Cici not giving it to anyone else.

MOMMY: And who came to see you Sunday night?

CHLOE: Big Kelly coming to see me for . . . What's it called?

MOMMY: To babysit.

CHLOE: And it was so fun. And thank you for my family, and one more thing, oh, thank you for Mallory, Daddy, and Mommy and everybody else in the world. Amen!

MOMMY: Nice job.

IN SICKNESS

Only Chloe could be happy about her very first sleepover that ended with her best friend throwing up, as well as her friend's older brother and sister. Children are like walking petri dishes. I've gotten over worrying about who is going to come home with what germs. But on this occasion, she woke up to discover that her friend had gotten sick and left the room, leaving her all alone in an unfamiliar house.

"Mommy, I didn't know what to do," she told me later. "Cici left and I was alone."

Previously, Chloe had only spent the night at relatives' homes, so the decision to allow her to attend her first real sleepover was not taken lightly. I asked her multiple times if she was okay with it, and she assured me she was. The big question was, was *I* okay with it? From a practical standpoint, I was. We had known the family for years, before the girls were even born. Chloe and Cici had become fast friends in kindergarten.

"Mommy, please let me do it," she had begged.

"Are you sure you're ready for this?" I said as if I were asking her if she was ready to drive a car.

"I'm sure."

Mallory was also going to a sleepover at a friend's house directly across the street from where Chloe was staying, so I knew that if Chloe had a problem, the mother could always call Mallory and have her come over and comfort her sister. But she is still my baby, so it was hard to let her go, even for one night.

"Mommy, Mallory will be close by if I need her," Chloe said, tugging on the bottom of my sweater, looking up at me with pleading eyes.

The next morning I received a text from Cici's mother explaining that all three of her children were throwing up and that we should probably come get Chloe. Of course, I jumped in the car and got there as fast as I could, imagining that Chloe would be upset about waking up in a strange room alone with her friend nowhere to be found. Amazingly, Chloe was in good spirits and told me she'd like to try a sleepover again sometime when Cici was *not* sick.

"Mommy, it will be much better the next time when she's not throwing up," Chloe said matter-of-factly as we drove home.

I was relieved that the experience didn't spoil her desire to go on a sleepover in the future. But it was just like Chloe to look at the bright side of things. I was proud of her. I was also relieved that she didn't get sick in light of her being in a house full of sick children.

As a mother, letting go is not an easy thing to do. I'm getting better at it, but it is still something I struggle with, especially with Chloe because she is my youngest. That's why, when I am not with my children, I literally picture the hands of God cradling them as they move through the world without me. At least if I can't always be there, I take comfort in the fact that he is.

CHLOE: Dear God and Jesus, thank you for me and Daddy handing out the Indian Princess invitations. And going to this work place where Daddy bought things for our new beach house, and I got to wear his hat and gloves that he had in the car and ride on this really fun thingy. You know those big things?

MOMMY: Like a loader?

CHLOE: Yeah, kind of.

MOMMY: That doesn't sound safe.

CHLOE: No, it's just like with wheels on it.

MOMMY: Is that when you got the mattresses?

CHLOE: No, that's when we got sink stuff, really big stuff. It was safe. They're kind of like carts. But they only have handles right here, they don't have anything right there.

MOMMY: That sounds dangerous.

CHLOE: But I had to hold on when I was in the street.

MOMMY: You were in the street?

CHLOE: No!

MOMMY: You're going to get Daddy in trouble.

CHLOE: I can't explain it. I don't know how to explain it.

MOMMY: I'll ask him, believe me, I'll ask him.

CHLOE: It's like when we were going to the car to bring our stuff. I don't know what it's called . . . Help.

MOMMY: Your family? Just thank you for your family. Thank you for the pretty snow.

CHLOE: Thank you for my Indian Princess thing in, like, three days. Sunday, today is Thursday.

MOMMY: So it's in, like, three days.

CHLOE: And thank you for my family, oh, and one more thing, thank you for everybody in the world. Amen.

The Best of Both Worlds

If there's one truism about the different ways women and men parent that is pretty much universal, it's the fact that mothers are overprotective and fathers are more relaxed. Case in point: the fact that Grif allowed Chloe to ride on some kind of massive cart at Home Depot was not something I would have approved of had I been there.

Chloe is aware that I don't always agree with what her father allows her to do, so she tries not to say anything to get him in trouble. Grif is also aware that I worry sometimes when she is with him that he doesn't employ the same safety practices that I do.

"Daddy, it will be our secret," I imagine her saying to him.

"That's right. Don't tell your mother," he responds with a finger to his lips in a hush gesture.

And while I wasn't really mad at Grif for allowing her to ride on the cart at Home Depot, I did question his judgment a little, especially when she said she drove it into the road. But at the heart of the matter is the fact that little girls trust their fathers to keep them safe. They also count on them for a little adventure in their lives. It's a delicate balance of a father's saying something is okay to do, and a child's assuming it is safe and following his lead. In this case, Chloe did something outside of her comfort zone, had a little adventure because she was with her daddy, and, therefore, felt safe. And in my heart I knew she was too.

This is why God gives children two parents—so they can have the best of both worlds.

CHLOE: Dear God and Jesus, thank you for all my animals being in a purple box and turning them all over so I can get out all the new animals I haven't used in a long time. [She is referring to her stuffed animals that she keeps in a purple plastic trunk.]

MOMMY: Good job.

CHLOE: Let's see. And thank you for Indian Princesses having a camping trip. And thank you for going skiing in, like, a week or something. And thank you for going to New Mexico just me and Mommy to meet one of her friends from college and her daughter that's going to be my friend. And thank you for my family, and one more thing, oh, thank you for Mommy. Amen.

Soul Vacation

I'm not really sure when the idea came to me that I wanted to take Chloe on a solo vacation, but when it did, I immediately knew I had made the right choice. Unlike her sister, who had enjoyed three years alone with her parents before Chloe came along, Chloe rarely, if ever, got one-on-one time with me, with the exception of our bedtime ritual. Most of our outings involved the entire family, or just me and both girls.

I decided to visit a dear friend from college whom I had not seen in years who happened to have a daughter Chloe's age. We had never met one another's children (with the exception of a brief trip she made east when Mallory was a newborn), and I had been to New Mexico, so I knew it was a beautiful place to visit. I imagined this would be a great mother-daughter adventure.

"Really, Mommy, just us, on an airplane together?" she asked with giddiness in her voice. Somehow, the airplane ride was ranking slightly higher than the actual vacation itself.

"Just us," I said as I tried to make her ponytails even—no easy task for a hairstyle-challenged mother.

The fact that Chloe was so excited about it—excited enough to continually mention it in her prayers leading up to the trip—made me feel so good. As parents we never really know what our children think of us, especially after they get out of the needy, cuddly stage, and their declarations of love become fewer and more subtle. And let's face it, it *does* matter to us. Even though we are supposed to be on the supply end of unconditional love, deep down inside, we want and need to know our children love us back in the same way.

"Mommy, it's going to be great. We should take lots of games and books to keep us busy on the plane. Do they have snacks on planes?" she asked, still consumed with the mode of travel.

On one hand I didn't want to talk about the trip too much because I didn't want Mallory to get upset, even though she was preparing to spend a week by herself getting spoiled by her grandmother, Maddie, in Pennsylvania. But just knowing how enthusiastic Chloe was about the trip was validation that I was doing something right—that my child was as thrilled about spending a week with me as I was about spending it with her. I prayed to God this would continue for many years to come.

5

REBIRTH

The day the Lord created hope was probably
the same day he created Spring.

—BERN WILLIAMS

CHLOE: Dear God and Jesus, thank you for getting little toy chicks, like little mini ones, and making Mommy's dinner tonight for Indian Princesses. You earn a feather for making your mom's dinner.

MOMMY: It was great. I loved it.

CHLOE: And Mommy liked it. The mom is supposed to write a letter about how it was. And thank you for my family, and one more thing, oh, thank you for Mallory, Sissy, Mommy, and Daddy, and everybody else. Amen.

TO SERVE

I had been through it before with Mallory. The girls in the Y-Princess tribe can earn their "feathers" by doing good deeds. One of the more common tasks they can undertake is making dinner for their mothers. As parents, we are so used to serving our children, serving our families, that when the tables are turned, it feels slightly unnatural and awkward.

I remember one time being down on my knees washing Chloe's feet with a wash cloth after she insisted on taking off her shoes and playing in a pile of dirt. I remember thinking that the humility required to parent is similar to the humility Jesus shows us. It is the same feeling I had another time when I was down on my knees clipping Mallory's little toenails as her tiny legs dangled from the toilet. A daunting thought washed over me—including my own, I am now responsible for *sixty* nails.

Chloe has always taken a particular joy in serving others. She is just now getting to the age when she can actually help around the house, and she loves it—from bringing in groceries, to picking up her room, to helping me clean, she is always willing to pitch in.

"Mommy, here is your menu, just so you know what you'll be having in case you don't know what it is," she said with an apron tied three times around her waist.

"Thank you, sweetie. I can't wait. I know it's going to be great," I said as I started to get up from the couch to reach for the menu.

"No, Mommy. Sit. Relax. This is *your* night," she said, coming toward me with the menu in one hand, her other palm up in stop-mode.

When it was time to eat, she gently took my hand and led me from the den to the table where I found tortellini, garlic bread, and salad, all of my favorite foods.

It wasn't the food that touched me, but the way Chloe stood by the table and beamed. She proudly watched my reaction as I surveyed what she had done for me and smiled, pulling her in for a hug. In that moment, I realized what an important lesson she was teaching me— that all the giving a mother does *is* recognized by her children, even if they don't always verbalize it. By giving freely to our children, they learn to give back to others. It's God's simple plan to make the world a better place.

MOMMY: What's wrong, baby?

CHLOE: I did it.

MOMMY: You didn't do it, I did it. I dropped it. It is no big deal. It's all fixed. Give Mama a prayer.

CHLOE: Dear God and Jesus, thank you for my friend's birthday, getting popsicles for the birthday. I had lemonade, green lemonade, limeade. Thank you for getting to go skiing. Seeing Allison tomorrow when I haven't seen her in a long, long time. And thank you for my family, and one more thing, oh, thank you for Mommy, Daddy, and Sissy, and everybody else. And no, Mommy, I don't love you just a little bit more than everybody (*grinning*). Amen.

Passing the Buck

Chloe was upset because she had accidentally knocked the digital recorder out of my hand and sent the batteries careening across the room. Luckily, there was no harm done. I was able to put it back together and it worked like a charm. But she was still crying, her head buried in the pillow, refusing to look at me because she felt ashamed and thought she had broken it.

"All my fault, Mommy," she said in between sobs.

"No, it was an accident. And it's fine. No worries," I said, stroking her little blond head, pulling the wet, matted strands away from her damp cheeks.

Chloe had always reacted this way when she thought she had done something wrong. It was a mix of sincere humiliation and sorrow for her perceived wrong. No matter how many times I told her not to worry about things that didn't matter, she still internalized what she considered to be bad behavior.

What occurred to me, however, was that she was taking a profound sense of responsibility for her actions in a way that in our pass-the-buck culture we have forgotten how to do. As adults, it is so much easier to blame others for our shortcomings than it is to take ownership of them. I was taught as a child to admit when I am wrong, but somewhere along the way I morphed into an adult who sometimes took this route and sometimes didn't. Chloe's humility has caused me to take another look at this issue. I now feel more committed than ever to doing the right thing and trying to always take responsibility for my actions even when I'm not proud of my behavior.

"You make me a better person, Chloe," I say to her often.

"Mommy, you're good just the way you are," she retorts.

As parents, sometimes we need to reevaluate our choices if we intend to be good examples to our children. Once again, Chloe was proving to me that doing the right thing was not a moment-by-moment choice, but a way of being that God intended us to live into.

CHLOE: Dear God and Jesus, thank you for going on a campout.

MOMMY: What did you do today?

CHLOE: And I had a playdate.

MOMMY: And you were sick, but you are better now.

CHLOE: Why would I put that in my prayer, that I was sick?

MOMMY: Because God made you better, didn't he?

CHLOE: No, he didn't, you never gave me the medicine.

MOMMY: Honey, there is no medicine for the stomach flu. You just have to get over it, but we cared for you. Mommy stayed up all night with you, remember that?

CHLOE: Thanks for getting to read three good Angel . . . Angelerina, Anglerna . . . books.

MOMMY: *Angelina*. It's hard to say, isn't it?

CHLOE: Stop. And thank you for my family, and one more thing, oh, thank you for Mallory, Mommy, Daddy, and everybody else. Amen.

BECAUSE I LOVE YOU

Even angels get crabby sometimes. On this night Chloe was in rare form. She was tired and fussy. Nothing I said appealed to her, from my suggestions of what to pray about to my *outrageous* idea that God had helped her recover from her brief illness.

"No," she grunts when she is annoyed by something I say. When she gets that way, I just have to sit back and wait for the foul mood to pass.

But for my glass-half-full girl, this is not the norm. I'm the one who is supposed to be crabby after ten hours in high heels with multiple unreasonable deadlines and more work to do after I put my children to bed. I was relying on her to be my ray of sunshine that would lighten my mood and prepare me for a long night of work ahead. But instead, I found myself being her cheerleader, mustering every last amount of energy reserves I had stored to try and turn her negative mood around.

"You know, Mommy sometimes feels this way after a hard day," I said to her after the prayer was done. She recoiled from my touch. So I put my hands in my lap and simply sat in the darkness of her room to let her know I wasn't going anywhere.

What amazed me was my patience. Somehow, at work, when my fuse gets short, I don't always employ the same diplomatic approach. Yet, in this situation, I think I was able to persevere with a positive attitude because Chloe had taught me how to do this on so many nights when I was feeling low and needed a pick-me-up.

"Why are you still here?" she asked in a muffled voice through her pillow that she had placed over her head.

"Because I love you."

And that's exactly why God is always there for us when we need him. Even when we don't always appear to appreciate his love, he keeps coming back for more. As parents, we stay, even when our child seems to be in a dark place. I was beginning to understand just how far I had come in the yearlong journey that started with a single prayer.

MOMMY: Chloe and I are getting really close to finishing our one hundred prayers. Chloe, do you want to give me a little prayer?

CHLOE: Thank you for getting to go back to school today.

MOMMY: What did you do tonight?

CHLOE: Read really good books and going to acting.

MOMMY: Was it fun to see Tina?

CHLOE: Kind of. Daddy didn't set the Wii up.

MOMMY: I'll talk to him.

CHLOE: And for Tina coming. And thank you for my family, and one more thing, oh, thank you for everybody in the world. Amen. Thank you for finding my Pet Shop Kitty.

PET SHOP KITTY

I guess you've probably figured out by now that nothing is too small to garner Chloe's undivided attention. While I tend to rush through life like a jet fighter, only stopping occasionally to refuel, Chloe stops frequently and notices all the little things.

Chloe's Pet Shop adoration started about a year ago when she realized these creatures would fit into her pocket. Her mild obsession also became the bane of my existence as I tried to keep track of all the little critters. I kept finding them all over the house, not to mention in the pocket of my robe, or in my raincoat, or at the bottom of my purse. I decided they must be breeding because they seemed to multiply daily.

While I couldn't tell one Pet Shop doll from the other, Chloe had names for each one, knew their gender, and even knew things like their favorite colors and whether they liked strawberries or camping. So when Pet Shop Kitty went MIA a few days prior to this prayer, the threat level in the house rose to DEFCON five. She was hysterical. I looked in all the usual places—beneath the couch cushions, beneath her pillows, in my pockets, in the dark depths of my purse, *nothing*. I told her we would get a new Pet Shop Kitty at the store. She informed me this was not possible because it was part of a larger set.

"Plus, Mommy, it's not about that. It's about Pet Shop Kitty being lost and scared," she said with sincere tears in her eyes. I kept looking every day, but I have to admit, I was skeptical. Our house is usually pretty well organized. I imagined that Pet Shop Kitty would have shown up by now if she was still around. I felt sure Chloe would forget about it, but I was wrong. She brought it up constantly.

"Mommy, have you found Pet Shop Kitty yet?" she asked as I trudged in the door, dropping my briefcase and three bags of groceries in the front hallway.

"No, sweetie, still looking hard, though," I said, wondering if I might be hit by lightning for lying to my child. Sure, I had looked, but it wasn't a priority. I had laundry to fold, a dishwasher to unload, lunches to pack, bills to pay, and books to write. Looking for Pet Shop Kitty was somewhere between organizing the last three years' worth of photos and cleaning out the camping gear we had not used in ten years.

"Mommy, she is probably so scared and hungry by now," Chloe moaned and wrapped her arms around my waist, burying her head in my stomach.

But miraculously, on this night, I threw on a fleece jacket that I had not worn in a long time, and there was Pet Shop Kitty, in my pocket. I had most likely picked her up one night on my daily evening sweep of the house for debris left over from our family's busy day. When I reached in the pocket of the jacket and felt the little hard plastic creature, I felt triumphant. It gave me great pleasure to be Chloe's saving grace.

"Oh, Mommy, thank you so much. I've been so worried about Pet Shop Kitty," she said, tenderly taking the blue plastic cat out of my hand and cradling it as if it were really alive.

For a brief moment, I was her hero again as I marveled at yet another miracle.

CHLOE: Dear God and Jesus, thank you for my family, and thank you for a couple minutes with my friends, because then it started raining. And thank you for . . . Help . . .

(*Mallory is interrupting in the background as she looks for a dress-up outfit in Chloe's closet.*)

MOMMY: Your first communion. That's dance recital stuff [to Mallory]. Go to the playroom and get something.

MALLORY: Will you come with me?

MOMMY: Let me finish the prayer.

CHLOE: Thank you for my first communion and getting to go to New Mexico with Mommy starting next Saturday. Help me . . .

MALLORY: (*whispering*) And thank you for Mallory.

MOMMY: Thank you for all the times you got to play with your friends and how Luke almost had a sleepover.

CHLOE: And Luke had half of a sleepover on Saturday night.

MALLORY: Why didn't you let him spend the night?

MOMMY: And we made Easter eggs.

CHLOE: And we made eggs.

MALLORY: And seeing a suspicious guy pour corn in the woods [to feed the deer], and we caught tadpoles.

CHLOE: We caught tadpoles and Miss Dina is going to grow them into frogs. We found, like, forty-two. And thank you for my family, and one more thing, oh, thank you for everybody in the whole world. Amen!

Triaging

Since the beginning of the prayer journey, Mallory had been intermittently miffed that Chloe and I had chosen to do something without her. Truth be told, we were more like the Three Musketeers when Grif wasn't around. We tended to do everything together. So it was no surprise that she was a little envious of this moment she wasn't sharing with us.

At first, when she would interrupt, I would get angry and send her out of the room. This would usually end badly with Mallory pouting in the other room and Chloe complaining about how her sister always interrupted our private moments. But slowly, I had learned how to handle these interruptions more deftly so they didn't completely derail the prayer process. It made me think about all the stopping and starting in my day as a news reporter where flexibility was paramount to success.

"She never lets us have one-on-one time," Chloe would say, spouting an adult phrase from who knows where.

But as the prayer journey went on, I became more adept at fielding Mallory's obvious attempts for attention. Rather than get upset with her, I tried to acknowledge her and let her know that I would help her and spend time with her when I was done with Chloe. It was similar to how I balanced competing projects at work—*triage*.

"Mallory deserves some time too, Chloe," I began to explain to her. "She doesn't mean to interrupt. She's just trying to get my attention and is not sure how to go about it."

"Okay, but can we lock the door when we do prayers from now on?" she would say.

My handling of these interruptions is still not seamless, but as I tried to understand where Mallory was coming from, putting myself in her shoes, it got easier. Life is full of interruptions, and with God's help I was getting much closer as a parent to learning how to field them at home with aplomb.

Chloe on Peace:

Peace is the love of God. Just think about it—it's beautiful.

MOMMY: Oh my goodness, we're tired girls. I had to work last night, and Chloe probably stayed up too late. Right? (*She shake's her head.*) You didn't? Okay.

CHLOE: No, like 8:23. I don't know. Probably like 9:15 or something.

MOMMY: Well, let's say a prayer.

CHLOE: Dear God and Jesus, thank you for . . . Help me . . .

MOMMY: Having your sister read you books.

CHLOE: Having Mallory read me books, to go to school again because the weekend was a couple days ago, a beautiful day, and getting to bring in my presentation to school in a couple of days.

MOMMY: In two days. That's going to be exciting.

CHLOE: Thank you for my family, and one more thing, oh, thank you for Mommy, Daddy, Sissy, and everybody else in the world. Amen.

NIGHT OWLS

Fighting the desire to skip the prayer and simply go to bed had become something I had made peace with. The prayer was now woven into the fabric of our lives like brushing teeth and reading a book before bed. I knew on this night that Chloe was as tired as I was because I had worked late the night before, and her dad wasn't the greatest at enforcing bedtime. All too often, I would be driving down my street at some ungodly hour from work, and I would see the lights go off in the girls' rooms as I pulled into the driveway. I would come in to find him out of breath in bed pretending he had been lazily watching television *alone*.

"Girls in bed?" I would ask with a smile.

"Yep," he would say with a fake yawn, as if they had been in bed for hours. I could see the little indentations on the bed next to him where they had no doubt been curled up watching *American Idol* or some old movie with him. I could hear the girls snickering beneath their covers from their bedrooms across the hall.

But as tired as I was, I realized that this prayerful moment with Chloe had become something I looked forward to at the end of each day. After all was said and done, after the yelling in my office, the negative e-mails from viewers, the cardiac arrest I almost experience daily as I met impossible deadlines, this moment had become my foundation, my bedrock, the moment each day that continually anchored me to what was really important.

"Young lady, I know you're still awake. I can hear you in there. Let's do a prayer," I would say, nuzzling Chloe's neck with my nose until she burst out laughing.

I had come to realize that while the words were important, more important was the time I was spending acknowledging my role as a parent, and yes, as ill equipped as I still feel that I am, as somewhat of a spiritual guide to my daughter. No, I don't have all the answers. In fact, I still have more questions than answers, but I am learning that giving my troubles over to God is not a bad way to go even when I'm almost too tired to tell him about them.

CHLOE: Dear God and Jesus, thank you for getting to play with my friends and getting this cool thing that you wave around. It's really cool and pretty. But I left it at my friend Brenna's house. And thank you for having Indian Princesses at Brenna's house.

MOMMY: What else did you do this weekend? Where did you go?

CHLOE: Thank you for going to the beach and seeing Vi.

MOMMY: What else did we do? Played tennis?

CHLOE: Played tennis.

MOMMY: We did long scooter rides.

CHLOE: We went on scooter rides.

MOMMY: And we went to the festival yesterday.

CHLOE: And going to the festival yesterday, and I got, like, a little toy trumpet.

MOMMY: Sounds like you had a pretty good weekend, and you got to stay up late. And what did you do last night?

CHLOE: And playing Bananagrams with Mommy and Daddy, because I went to bed three hours early because I was so tired, because the other night I stayed up late and then—

MOMMY: And then you woke up and played a game with us.

CHLOE: And then I woke up, and I stayed up really late, and then I got to sleep with Mommy. Thank you for my family and one more thing, oh, thank you for Mommy and everybody else in the world. Amen!

MOMMY: That was beautiful.

Stolen Moments

One of my earliest memories as a child is sneaking down late at night into the den and watching the news with my father. I would sit quietly cuddled up next to him in his big blue arm chair. The deal was that I couldn't talk and interrupt his television viewing, and he wouldn't tell my mom I was up because she would surely shoo me right back to bed. He had a tray next to him that contained the same thing every night—a mug of cold beer, a cigar, and three Oreo cookies. This was the 1970s, after all; no one had concerns about things like second-hand smoke and cholesterol. If I was lucky, he would share an Oreo with me in return for my obedient silence.

On this particular night, Chloe had passed out on the couch after a daylong street festival at the beach near her grandmother's house. We had carried her to bed shortly after that. Mallory had also gone to bed relatively early. My husband and I were enjoying having a rare evening without children. We decided to play one of our new favorite word games—Bananagrams. A little after ten that night we heard some noise in the hallway and turned around to see Chloe clad in her blue fuzzy robe and slippers, her little blond mane askew, with a Cheshire cat grin across her face.

"I can't sleep," she said sheepishly.

"Well, come on in," I said, waving her over, not having the strength to deny such cuteness.

It was obvious from the beginning that she felt like she was getting away with something, breaking the rules by staying up so late. My mother's voice inside my head told me to put her back to bed, but the memory of those special late nights with my father discouraged that thought.

"Just one game, Mommy. Okay?" she said, unfairly batting her big blue eyes at me. But don't be deceived; she is a fierce competitor when it comes to word games.

"One game, young lady. And then it's right to bed. Promise?"

"Promise," she replied as she was already gathering her seventeen letters in her corner of the table.

I was beginning to understand there is never a wasted moment with a child. Unwittingly, Chloe was teaching me about carving out time from my chaotic life to get to the heart of what really mattered. It's a lesson that all parents need to learn, and relearn, as their children enter each new stage of life. I was learning that God intended for me to prioritize these precious moments in my life above everything else, and that if I could do that, the half-full glass was within my reach.

CHLOE: I don't want to talk, Mommy. Daddy used all my voice.

MOMMY: Daddy used all your voice? How did he do that?

CHLOE: I had to yell at him so much.

MOMMY: What did you have to yell at him about?

CHLOE: Can't talk.

MOMMY: You said you had to tell him to wear a seatbelt?

CHLOE: I don't know. How can I remember?

MOMMY: How about I talk about the things you told me?

CHLOE: Do all the things I told you.

MOMMY: Dear God and Jesus, Chloe would like to thank you for some of the things she did at Indian Princesses because they were really fun. She loved the zip line.

CHLOE: It was fifty feet high.

MOMMY: It was fifty feet high.

CHLOE: Over water, and then you go in to where there are turtles. But I didn't get near turtles.

MOMMY: But you did chase some turtles?

CHLOE: I tried to chase turtles.

MOMMY: How many did you see? You said you saw ninety-nine.

CHLOE: Almost.

MOMMY: Almost ninety-nine. You did BB guns. You got to shoot BB guns, which you didn't tell me at first, because you thought I would be mad because you know I don't like guns, right?

CHLOE: Daddy told me not to tell.

MOMMY: He told you not to tell? You had a big camp fire. That was cool.

CHLOE: One of the men helping out, he sang "Little Bunny Foo Foo," and we had to copy him. He said, "Loud. We need you to scream!" He said, "Little Bunny Foo Foo hopping through the forest, scooping up the field mice and bopping them on the head." He said, "Now make sure you bop your dads on the head!"

MOMMY: That's funny.

CHLOE: Then he said, "Little Bunny Foo Foo, pick up the field mice and bop them on the head or I'll turn you into a goon!"

MOMMY: And you found sharks' teeth?

CHLOE: I found sharks' teeth.

MOMMY: Archery.

CHLOE: Oh, I had archery.

MOMMY: You had a ghost story.

CHLOE: My ghost story—I don't want to talk about that.

MOMMY: Let's not talk about that. You had Krispy Kreme donuts.

CHLOE: Three for breakfast.

MOMMY: You got to be with all your friends, all your buddies from Indian Princesses. Then you got to go to a baseball game today.

CHLOE: Going to a baseball game to listen to Mallory sing the national anthem.

MOMMY: Who did you see there?

CHLOE: Cari Beth.

MOMMY: No, you brought Cari Beth with you.

CHLOE: I saw my cousin, the cutest kid in the world.

MOMMY: What's her name?

CHLOE: Sydney.

MOMMY: She is cute. She loved you.

CHLOE: She is the cutest baby in the world.

MOMMY: She's your cousin.

CHLOE: She's so cute.

MOMMY: She is. She likes you.

CHLOE: Remember the last time she was like, "Goo goo."

MOMMY: Now she can talk.

CHLOE: You know little babies, when they can't walk or not say anything. That's not fun, that's exciting only for the mom.

MOMMY: Do you want to thank God for your family?

CHLOE: Thank you for my family, and one more thing, oh, thank you for Mommy. I'm not talking good because I lost my voice, because I had to scream at Daddy because he wasn't wearing a seatbelt. I lost all of my voice now. Amen.

Guiding Light

Chloe's husky voice told me all I needed to know about her camping trip with her father. She had had a blast and was absolutely wiped out. On top of that, Mallory's choir had sung the national anthem at a local baseball game the day that Chloe had attended, so she was truly double-wiped.

"You lost your voice? Who took it?" I asked her jokingly when she told me that night her voice was "missing."

"Probably a bad guy," she said with a grin and her trademark sarcasm that was developed well beyond her six years.

The thing that had made me so impatient in the beginning of the prayer journey, having to guide Chloe's prayers, had become seamless without me consciously acknowledging it. I knew about her day because she had excitedly shared the details with me when she returned from the trip. So when it came time to pray, I was ready to help her with things to pray about.

In the beginning of the prayer journey, her inability to focus would have made me frustrated to the point where I might have simply ended it. But after a year of saying prayers with her night after night, I had evolved into her capable guide. Without even knowing it, I had become a leader in the development of my child's spirituality, and no doubt in my own at the same time.

"Mommy, can you just say it for me?" she would say when she was so tired she could barely keep her eyes open.

"I sure will, sweetie."

Chloe's biggest concern every night was always leaving someone, or something, out. So I made a mental checklist of all the exciting things I knew she had done at camp—zooming down the zip line, shooting the BB gun, hearing ghost stories around the camp fire. Instead of maneuvering the prayer with annoying, anxious prompts, I slowly wove the elements of her weekend into the tapestry of the prayer. Looking back on all Chloe did in the past year, in a weekend, in a single day, I know that she is a blessed child to have so many friends and so many fun activities in her life. I, too, am blessed to be part of providing that life for her—a life where she is exposed to so many different opportunities.

So, while I am by no means a certified spiritual guide, I feel that I have graduated from a part-timer to a full-timer with God's help.

CHLOE: Dear God and Jesus, thank you for going and watch Mallory sing the national anthem at the baseball game. Thank you for going roller-skating with my friends outside.

MOMMY: And what did you have tonight?

CHLOE: Having acting tonight. That was my practice before my real show. Who is coming to my show?

MOMMY: Daddy. I have a book signing.

CHLOE: And thank you for . . . Help . . .

MOMMY: Maybe something you missed from Indian Princesses. Did you miss any of the cool stuff that you did there?

CHLOE: Oh yeah, when you do all the things you have a ticket to know what you have. They give you letters, and you unscramble them and you get a gold thing on your ticket. You finished your whole ticket. You got to get sixteen, and we did. And thank you for seeing Anna, Taylor, Nisma, Eden.

MOMMY: You saw all those girls at Indian Princesses?

CHLOE: Yes, besides my tribe. And of course Brenna, Cara, Cari Beth, Jordan, Cici, because they are in my tribe.

MOMMY: What about your family?

CHLOE: Thank you for my family, oh, one more thing, thank you for Mommy, Daddy, and Sissy. Amen!

With a Little Help from My Friends

You've gathered by now that Chloe is a social butterfly. She is never happier than when she is playing with a friend or a group of friends. She has no concerns about age, race, or even gender most of the time. Chloe likes anyone who likes her and is very conscious of not ever leaving anyone out. God's love is always shining brightly through her.

"I don't not like anyone," she said to me. "There are just some people I like more than others." That's why in this prayer she wanted to name everyone in her class that she had run into on her camping trip with her dad. Her pattern of collecting friends has made me realize that Chloe treasures each individual friendship. While I also feel this way about my friendships, longstanding and new, I don't always express this to my friends. I have neglected important long-term friendships. Children, work, and distance have gotten in the way and become excuses for less contact with them. The truth is that when I do reconnect with these friends, I find it so fulfilling. In the words of Bob Seger, "See some old friends, good for the soul." It is almost hard to explain what it's like to share a laugh and stay up all night talking with a friend you love, but haven't seen in years. It feeds you in ways that are beyond definition.

"Chloe, you are a good friend," I tell her on a regular basis. "That's a really great quality in a person." And I mean it. She is a good friend, and she inspires me to do better in this area.

Sure, we're all on Facebook together, but I'm looking for more meaningful interaction. I've decided that the next time a friend invites me to an important event in her family's life, I won't find excuses not to go. I will simply make it happen. It's not unusual at this point in a busy mother's life to have lost touch with friends, but I think now is the time to rekindle those soul-fulfilling relationships. When we do, we often have a new friend or two in tow for our friends' children to meet—our children. And so the circle remains unbroken.

CHLOE: Dear God and Jesus, thank you for . . . I don't know.

MOMMY: You had ballet today. That was fun.

CHLOE: Going to ballet and reading good books.

MOMMY: I saw your roller skates outside. Did you go roller-skating a little bit?

CHLOE: Oh my gosh, I have to bring them inside because it's raining!

MOMMY: I brought them inside. I brought them inside.

CHLOE: And thank you for roller-skating outside today. We've been doing that a lot because Connor and Brooke have been doing it. And thank you for it being a nice day today and going back to school today from the weekend and almost ending the school and going to second grade. And thank you for my family, and one more thing, oh, thank you for Mommy. Amen.

BEGINNINGS

Springtime is always a gateway to pure beauty in North Carolina. While my kids play outside year-round, the spring is absolute perfection here. It is the beginning of a glorious temperate season where the colors pop all around you like vivid images in an abstract painting and the sun shines so brightly you literally feel it on the inside. It happens almost overnight. One morning you are shivering in your house, cranking up the heat and searching for a sweater; the next minute you step out to get the paper and the dogwoods are blooming, and everything is green and lush around you.

"Mommy, I love it when the flowers finally come out," Chloe said to me one day as we were passing a row of bright yellow daffodils in full bloom. "'Cause I know summer is just around the corner."

By this time of year, Chloe and Mallory are already in a cycle of playing outside until dark with their friends. On weekends, they get outside as fast as they can after they wake up to enjoy the beautiful weather. When they were young, I was often outside with them. Back then, it felt like I was wasting time. Now I know the truth: that I was enjoying God's creation and had an excuse to do so. Now I'm back to my old adult ways—spending a beautiful day inside organizing a closet or in front of my computer.

"Mommy, don't you ever get bored of sitting inside on the computer? Wouldn't you rather play outside with me?" Chloe said, cocking her head in one direction and her hip in the other.

"Yes, that would be great, but I've got a deadline, honey," I said, without looking up from the computer screen.

"Then I don't want to grow up if it's going to be like that," she retorted and turned to run back outside with her friends.

As I heard Chloe talk about heading to second grade on this night, it made me realize that there would only be so many springtimes left to enjoy with my children. Second grade would become seventh grade, and then college, and so on. We had begun the prayer journey just as Chloe was finishing kindergarten and beginning first grade, and now she was finishing first grade and beginning second grade in just a few short months. It is hard to believe that my baby is growing up. Along the way, I've grown up some too, reorganizing my priorities, dedicating myself not only to this journey but to writing something that I love, that inspires me, and that I hope will inspire others. This is a big departure for me.

"Does the invitation still stand to play?" I asked her on the heels of her declaration about not wanting to grow up.

"Sure, Mommy." She grabbed my hand and pulled me toward the front door.

God willing, there will be more springtimes in my life, and in the life of my child, but second grade will only come once for her, and it will be gone in the blink of an eye. I hope that I will practice what I have learned throughout this journey: to stop and pay attention to the beginnings instead of always focusing on the endings.

CHLOE: Dear God and Jesus, thank you for . . . Help . . .

MOMMY: Let's see, what did you do today at school, anything cool? Anything fun?

CHLOE: Going to PE and going to music, reading really good books with Mallory.

MOMMY: And who is coming to your class tomorrow?

CHLOE: And Mommy coming to class tomorrow to read books. And on our field trip.

MOMMY: Zoo field trip.

CHLOE: When is that?

MOMMY: May 12.

CHLOE: May 12, that's close to my birthday.

MOMMY: Yes, it is after your birthday.

CHLOE: Thank you for May 12, going to the zoo, and Mommy is coming with us.

MOMMY: And you're getting to go to the school carnival.

CHLOE: And thank you for my family, and one more thing, oh, thank you for Mommy, Daddy, and everybody else in the whole world. Amen.

TIME EQUALS LOVE

In the beginning of this journey, I asked myself over and over, "What does my child need from me?" I came up with a list. There are the basic things like food and shelter. Then there are more abstract concepts like spiritual and moral guidance. Then there is the overall umbrella of love. I love my children. I take care of them, and I tell them all the time just how much I love them. But at the end of the day, nothing shows your children you love them more than giving them your time.

"Mommy, you're always working," Chloe says to me often. "Work, work, work, work, work." When she says this, it gets my attention—*for the moment*. I usually stop and try to do something fun with her. But it's easy to slip back into old habits, where work ranks higher than playing with Barbies.

When children are very young, giving them time is a necessity because they cannot take care of themselves, but as they become a little bit older and more independent, it becomes easier for parents to pull away and give their kids more space. This is what we think they need and want, but, in reality, children always still want their parents' attention.

"Will you stay a little girl forever and always be my baby?" I ask Chloe all the time as I cuddle with her in bed at night.

"Mommy, I will always be your baby, but I will just be bigger. I have to grow up," she tells me.

This journey has taught me that in just a few short minutes every day I can develop a bond with my daughter, both one of love and of spirituality. Now I want to apply this concept to other aspects of my family's life. Hearing how excited she was about me reading in her class and driving on the field trip made me realize that I need to do more of this. Time equals love to children. I have always known this, but now I believe it deep down in my soul and want to make it a real presence in my life. God shows us, his children, unconditional love, and that is the same type of love we need to show to our own children.

The other day I worked it out so that I could go to a school play Chloe was in that I had previously thought I might have to miss. As soon as she saw me in the audience, she beamed. She leaned over to her friend and "whispered" loudly, "My mom is here." That set the tone for my entire day. All is right with the world when you've got God and Chloe on your side.

Chloe on Family:

My family protects me. They love me. Family won't hurt you no matter what. I would not want to be with anyone else but my family.

CHLOE: Dear God and Jesus, thank you for having my birthday in four days and getting to Hula Hoop, having a face painter, having some cake, and doing foam animals and doing trampoline and swings at my birthday.

MOMMY: And how was your weekend?

CHLOE: And thank you for going on a boat at the beach. I got to go on a boat, see Vi, go to a party, go to play at my friend's, the cutest girl in the world named Gracie. I hope the people in this place—the oil company spilled a lot of oil in the pond, they don't know how to clean it up. I hope they're okay.

MOMMY: Who told you about that?

CHLOE: It was on TV in our breakfast place, and Daddy told me. I hope this place that I think that blew up, I hope most of the people didn't get hurt, and I'm sorry for the people that did get hurt. Thank you for my family, and one more thing, thank you for Mommy. This is my last prayer. Amen. And my family.

AND GOD SO LOVED THE WORLD

There were really three beings on this journey—me, Chloe, and God. But like the famous poem by Mary Stevenson says, there was only one set of footprints. That's because while I was carrying my child, God was carrying both of us.

"The times when you have seen only one set of footprints, is when I carried you," God says in Stevenson's poem.

And so, on our journey to a better understanding of faith, love, and the bond between a parent and child, God carried us both as we learned together and grew.

On this night, Chloe knew the documented journey was ending, although our prayer life that had become rich and devout was really just beginning. Still, there was sadness for both of us as we realized the prayer project was coming to a close. We would still for years to come, I hope, lie quietly in the darkness together, sharing pieces of our day and thanking God for all the blessings in our lives. But from now on, it would be just me and her alone with no flashing red light from a digital recorder in my hand.

"It's kind of sad," she said to me in the following days.

"What's sad?"

"That it's over. My prayers."

"Your prayers aren't over, honey. We're just not recording them anymore," I told her. Her face lit up at this new revelation.

It was fitting that Chloe would end with her concerns about the victims of the 2010 Gulf oil spill. Her love and compassion for others never wavered throughout the year we spent documenting her prayers, and it inspired me greatly. It made me realize that only in looking outside of ourselves can we truly do what God calls us to do, which is to love the world.

God works through us to love the world; he worked through Chloe to show me how. I can honestly say without reservation that she's showing me what it means to love to God and back.

Epilogue:
Letters to God—
May 21, 2011

It was a beautiful early summer day along the North Carolina coast. The sky was robin's egg blue, full of white wispy clouds that if you stopped and looked closely resembled a cowboy, abstract ducks, and furry dogs. The soft, warm sand drifted through my toes—a sweet familiar reminder of the joy I always felt when walking close to the ocean. Chloe's little fingers were intertwined in mine, her silver sparkly nail polish glistened in the sunlight.

"I love the feeling of your hand in mine," I said, looking down at her. She beamed, squeezing my hand even tighter.

"Mommy, what is that?" she said, pointing to a mailbox that was literally coming out of a dune. Around it was a little wooden platform full of shells. Above it there were shells on fishing lines dangling from small plants at the edge of the dunes. I had probably walked by the same spot two dozen times in the previous year and never noticed the mailbox.

"I don't know. Let's check it out," I said as she released my hand and started to run toward our interesting find. As I got closer, I realized what it was. There were small handwritten notes resting beneath the shells. Some looked new. Others were yellowed and frayed, and the ink had run down the pages from spending too much time in the elements. The notes were all different, signed and dated by individual people. But they all had one thing in common: they were addressed to God. Some were thankful for "summer," "the blue sky," or "the ocean." Others asked for help for "tornado victims," for "tsunami victims," or for their own personal needs such as "healing my father." There were inspirational notes meant for passersby urging people to "hang in there" and to "believe in God's love." People had also carved and written notes to God in the wood all over the platform—notes that appeared to have been there for years.

I opened the mailbox and found a small notebook and a pen. There were some notes in the notebook, but there was also a large amount of blank paper left where someone could write a new note. I asked Chloe if she wanted to write a note and she did. She took the notebook and pen from me and walked away where she could lean on part of the wooden platform surrounding the magical spot. It was clear that she didn't want my curious eyes gazing over her shoulder as she wrote her note to God. After a few minutes she brought the notebook back. She had torn off the note and wanted to lay it out on the platform with shells surrounding it. I asked her if I could read it now, and she said yes.

God, I love you more than anything else, more than myself. May God be with you and also with me in my heart. Love, Chloe

Before her signature, Chloe drew a heart with an arrow through it. She proudly laid her note out on the worn wooden plank and delicately placed shells around its border to keep it from blowing away. She stood back and examined it, tipping the brim of her blue baseball hat up so that she could fully see her handiwork. She smiled and reached out for my hand, intertwining the sparkly nails in between my fingers again. I squeezed her hand and smiled as she looked up at me with a knowing grin well beyond her barely eight years.

"Chloe, I think your note is going to be a bright spot in someone's day. Strangers will read it, and it will make them smile, maybe even help them get through a rough patch, and you'll never know who it is that you touched," I said, pulling her in for a sandy, wet bathing suit hug.

In that moment it became clear to me that the journey we had started together was still ongoing. We had come to this sacred spot in the middle of a sandy, overgrown dune for a reason. This moment was proof to me that Chloe and I had both grown spiritually, that we had come to a place both literally, on this small North Carolina island, and figuratively, on our prayer journey, where we realized that prayer was about something much greater than ourselves. It was about the power of prayer to make the world around us a better place.

Ironically, I had walked by the mailbox so many times without seeing it—but finally, it took Chloe to show me the way. Not unlike the journey we had embarked on in May 2009, she had shown me how to become a more engaged mother and how to be more invested in my spiritual life. I picked up the pen and took the notebook and decided to write my own letter. For the first time in a long time I felt like I had something to say out loud to God. What I wrote is between me, Chloe, and God.

POSTSCRIPT

In August 2011, aggressive waves from an unusually high tide destroyed God's mailbox and the surrounding platform. The notes and the broken pieces of wood were washed out to sea. One day, while walking on the beach, we found what we thought was simply a faded piece of driftwood, but as we looked closer we realized it was covered with notes to God. The girls begged me to take it home. It is now in Chloe's room as a reminder that God hears all of our voices.

Prayer Primer
for Parents

Starting something new can be as difficult for parents as it is for children. Our busy lives often make creating a new discipline hard to imagine. But the richness of a daily prayer moment between you, your child, and God will create a new dimension, a peace in your life that helps to transcend all the chaos. It starts with one simple step—a commitment to do it every night. Once the pattern is established, you will be surprised by how much you and your child look forward to your prayer time. It becomes a focal point for the end of your day, and something you will always cherish, even as your child begins to develop his or her independent prayer life. Below are some simple guidelines to help you get started on the journey.

Easy Steps to Praying with Your Child

1. Pick a Time: Set aside a specific time to say a prayer with your child every night. Try to be consistent.

2. Pick a Place: Create a quiet, comfortable, peaceful atmosphere in which to pray with your child (in bed, low light, door closed).

3. Plan the Prayer: First discuss the purpose of prayer with your child. For example, thanking God, or asking for God's help. Give your child an example of a free-form prayer, especially if he or she is used to doing prayers by rote. Understand that speaking directly to God out loud, even if your mother or father is the only one in the room, can be intimidating to a young child.

4. Create an Opening: Come up with an opening together for the prayer. For example: "Dear God and Jesus." This helps you signal to your child that it's time to settle down and begin. It also makes the process less intimidating for children because they have a familiar starting point every night.

5. Give Your Child the Reins: Let your child begin the prayer, but prompt him or her when necessary. For example: "Are there good things that happened today that you want to thank God for? Is there anyone in our life who is hurting and needs God's help that we should pray for?"

6. Be Patient: If your child gets stuck or frustrated, tell him or her that God doesn't have a specific plan people need to follow when they pray. Guide, don't push. Only step in when your child asks for help. Silent moments during the prayer should not be considered obstacles, but moments of quiet reflection.

7. Thank God for Those You Love: At the end of the prayer ask your child to think about the people in his or her life that he or she wants to specifically thank God for. It can be family, friends, pets—anyone within your child's circle of love.

8. Create a Closing: Come up with a closing together. For example: "Thank you for my family. Amen." This will help your child know prayer time is over and it's time to go to

sleep. This can be especially useful when your child is tired and struggling and needs to be guided toward a conclusion.

9. Document Your Prayer Life: Keep a journal of the topics you and your child pray about for thirty days, and then review it to see how he or she is growing spiritually. Ask yourself, is my child becoming more comfortable with the process? Is there anything I can do to make my child more comfortable?

10. Relax and Enjoy: Now that you have made prayer a regular part of your life and your child's life, relax and enjoy the tradition you have created. Remember, it isn't about the length of the prayer, or whether or not it is profound or grammatically correct; it is about sharing your child's heart with God.

PRAYER STARTERS

Sometimes figuring out how to begin a prayer is the most difficult part of the process. A Bible verse can be a helpful prompt for your child, giving him or her something to think about. First, read the verse to your child or have your child read the verse to you and ask what he or she thinks it means. Then discuss the possible meanings of the verse together. Ask your child to use the lesson as background or context for the prayer.

1. For God so loved the world that he gave his one and only Son, that whoever believes in him shall not perish but have eternal life. (John 3:16)

DISCUSS: What does it mean to you that God gave us Jesus, that he sacrificed his Son for us?

PRAYER: Let's thank God for everything he does for us, including giving us eternal life.

2. But Jesus called the children to him and said, "Let the little children come to me, and do not hinder them, for the kingdom of God belongs to such as these." (Luke 18:16)

DISCUSS: Why do you think children are special to God?

PRAYER: Let's thank God for putting his hands beneath children and keeping them safe.

3. For he will deliver the needy who cry out, the afflicted who have no one to help. (Psalm 72:12)

DISCUSS: Why is it so important to God that we help people in need?

PRAYER: Are there people in your life or in the world in need that you want to ask God to help?

4. The earth is the LORD's, and everything in it, the world, and all who live in it. (Psalm 24:1)

DISCUSS: Who does God love? People? Animals? Plants?

PRAYER: Name some of the things in God's creation that you want to thank him for—for example, dogs, sunshine, your friends.

5. Neither height nor depth, nor anything else in all creation, will be able to separate us from the love of God that is in Christ Jesus our Lord. (Romans 8:39)

DISCUSS: How much do you love God? Why do you love God so much?

PRAYER: Thank God for his love and ask him to work through you to help you love others more.

6. God is our refuge and strength, an ever-present help in trouble. (Psalm 46:1)

DISCUSS: Think about times in your life, tough times, when you really need God.

PRAYER: Thank God for being there in those difficult times, and ask him to continue to be there when life gets hard.

7. The LORD is my light and my salvation—whom shall I fear? (Psalm 27:1)

DISCUSS: Talk about things you are afraid of—for example, the dark, taking a test at school, making new friends. Discuss how God can help take away our fears.

PRAYER: Thank God for helping you to be strong and confident in your life every single day.

8. This is the day the LORD has made; let us rejoice and be glad in it. (Psalm 118:24)

DISCUSS: Why do you think it's important to have a positive attitude every day? Do you have one? What could you do to be more positive?

PRAYER: Thank God for everything that makes our lives special and wonderful every day.

ACKNOWLEDGMENTS

I would like to thank my family—my husband, Grif, and my daughters, Mallory and Chloe—for their love and patience and for giving me the creative space to follow my dreams in the midst of our very busy lives.

I also would like to thank my parents for giving me a spiritual foundation on which to build throughout my life. Without their guidance, the journey to faith would not be possible.

As always, I need to thank my tireless agent, Sharlene Martin, for believing in me, and believing that I have many stories to tell that reflect many different parts of my life.

Thank you to my editors at Thomas Nelson, Bryan Norman and Heather Skelton, for shepherding this labor of love through its paces into something I am truly proud of.

And of course I need to thank God for giving me a child with light in her eyes and love in her heart.

AMANDA LAMB

ABOUT THE AUTHOR

Amanda Lamb is a professional television journalist with twenty-two years of experience. She covers the crime beat for an award-winning CBS affiliate in the southeast. Amanda is also the author of six books, a wife, and the mother of two little girls. She writes in two completely different genres—parenting memoir and true crime. In true crime, she has published *Love Lies* (2011, The Berkeley Group), *Evil Next Door* (2010, The Berkeley Group), and *Deadly Dose* (2008, The Berkeley Group). In parenting, Lamb has published *I Love You to God and Back* (2012, Thomas Nelson), *Girls Gone Child* (2011), and *Smotherhood* (2007, Globe Pequot).

Amanda received her undergraduate degree from Duke University and her master's degree in journalism from Northwestern University. For more details about Amanda and her writing go to www.alambauthor.com.

i Love you
TO GOD AND BACK
A BEDTIME PRAYER BOOK

amanda lamb
ILLUSTRATED BY POLONA LOVSIN

978-1-4003-2082-0 • $12.99

Show your precious little ones how much you love them ... with every bedtime prayer.

Starting with sweet and silly text about bedtime routines, this delightful book will then teach children how to pray: love God, ask Him for forgiveness, thank Him for many blessings, and offer requests. This unique story will make bedtime prayers a real learning and bonding experience for parents and children.

This complement to Amanda's beautiful book for grown-ups is a perfect bedtime book for parents and children.

www.thomasnelson.com